IN THE PINES

ALSO BY ALICE NOTLEY

165 Meeting House Lane ◆ 1971

Phoebe Light ◆ 1973

Incidentals in the Day World ◆ 1973

For Frank O'Hara's Birthday ◆ 1976

Alice Ordered Me to Be Made ◆ 1976

A Diamond Necklace ◆ 1977

Songs for the Unborn Second Baby ◆ 1979

Dr. Williams' Heiresses ◆ 1980

When I Was Alive ◆ 1980

How Spring Comes ◆ 1981

Waltzing Matilda ◆ 1981, REISSUED 2003

Tell Me Again ◆ 1982

Sorrento ◆ 1984

Margaret & Dusty ◆ 1985

Parts of a Wedding ◆ 1986

At Night the States ◆ 1988

From a Work in Progress ◆ 1988

Homer's Art ◆ 1990

The Scarlet Cabinet (with Douglas Oliver) ◆ 1992

To Say You ◆ 1993

Selected Poems of Alice Notley ◆ 1993

Close to me & Closer . . . (The Language of Heaven) and Désamère ◆ 1995

The Descent of Alette ◆ 1996

etruscan reader vii (with Wendy Mulford and Brian Coffey) ◆ 1997

Mysteries of Small Houses ◆ 1998

Byzantine Parables ◆ 1998

Disobedience ◆ 2001

Iphigenia ◆ 2002

From the Beginning ◆ 2004

Coming After: Essays on Poetry ◆ 2005

City Of ◆ 2005

Alma, or The Dead Women ◆ 2006

Grave of Light: New and Selected Poems 1970–2005 ◆ 2006

[IN THE PINES]

ALICE NOTLEY

PENGUIN POETS

PENGUIN BOOKS
Published by the Penguin Group
Penguin Group (USA) Inc.,
375 Hudson Street, New York, New York 10014, U.S.A.
Penguin Group (Canada), 90 Eglinton Avenue East, Suite 700, Toronto, Ontario,
Canada M4P 2Y3 (a division of Pearson Penguin Canada Inc.)
Penguin Books Ltd, 80 Strand, London WC2R 0RL, England
Penguin Ireland, 25 St Stephen's Green, Dublin 2, Ireland
(a division of Penguin Books Ltd)
Penguin Group (Australia), 250 Camberwell Road, Camberwell, Victoria 3124,
Australia (a division of Pearson Australia Group Pty Ltd)
Penguin Books India Pvt Ltd, 11 Community Centre, Panchsheel Park,
New Delhi–110 017, India
Penguin Group (NZ), 67 Apollo Drive, Rosedale, North Shore 0632,
New Zealand (a division of Pearson New Zealand Ltd.)
Penguin Books (South Africa) (Pty) Ltd, 24 Sturdee Avenue, Rosebank,
Johannesburg 2196, South Africa

Penguin Books Ltd, Registered Offices:
80 Strand, London WC2R 0RL, England

First published in Penguin Books 2007

Page vii constitutes an extension of this copyright page.

LIBRARY OF CONGRESS CATALOGING-IN-PUBLICATION DATA
Notley, Alice, 1945–
In the pines / Alice Notley.
p. cm.—(Penguin poets)
ISBN: 978-0-14-311254-9
I. Title.
PS3564.O7915 2007
811'.54—dc22   2007012076

Set in Sabon
Designed by Ginger Legato

146028962

Two excerpts from the work "In the Pines" were first published in the *American Poetry Review*. Certain poems were first published in *Pharos*, the *Philadelphia Independent*, *Jacket, McSweeney's,* and *Bed*. "Hemostatic" and "Our Violent Times" were published as broadsides by the Poetry Project and the University of Maine at Orono, respectively. Section 14 from the poem "In the Pines" was first published in the book *Grave of Light*.

For my sons and their friends

CONTENTS

IN THE PINES

In the Pines

I

Why should I respect, or convince, or even interest you? (Respect, conviction and interest belong to *him*.) On earth. Where we except for those in charge are drained from giving ourselves to each other until there's nothing left. In the year of our President. Eighteen coaches long.

There is no earth. There was no creation, there is no evolution nothing ever said by a then or a now *one*—their 19th century minds. Backwater rising come on.

The only thing you need to know here is whether or not you can stand my voice. Of which there is surely no such thing.

It is tones of bursting out but I can't *have* it, because it's composed of my inheritance and situation. That is a 19th century suit thought a black waistcoat and beard.

I may be trying to destroy you in order to live. I may only be trying to love you.

Jack of diamonds is a hard card, why should there be a story?

It's too hard a card to please, and it isn't the no earth I know. I got hepatitis C from shooting speed thirty-three years ago. But that isn't a story. Why are you continuing to read?

If you detest everything about your society, you say, why are you writing?

It is time to change writing completely.

You are not doing that.

Wait and see.

You have no stamina, you're a sick weakling.

◆　　◆　　◆

No one's calling me
to salvation or under
standing. who I am

on the old burnt ground, my baby.
the old burnt ground is my baby

facing a taller woman. I've never come this far before

The closet's in flames but he
lies dead in front of it. Staring

I am losing my because.
I said I was
the new species: no one.

♦   ♦   ♦

Momma don't treat your daughter mean.

There are tricks to writing novels, of no interest because the story loves whatever people do.

I hate whatever people do.

I am a real rat, unclear to myself, because there's no earth and no story. Unless I *am* a lab rat, experimented upon by people like men, so that I can do their will. Within the rat I am light which is bleak but the cast is disappearing so I can cease to become.

There are also tricks to writing poems, of no interest because poets tinker. On the cutting edge. Which isn't important unless it's the cooling board.

Kill it
for the human
area is over.

I feature him. who?
any love you'd.
deny it, all that love.
but I can't.

There's that thing of interest thing. "Interest" belongs, as I said,
to him too: something is of *interest* if the *he* structure says so.

I was not the taller woman. I have no more woman in me. I once
heard a man say he had a woman within, but how could he if I didn't?
They said, all writing is a translation.

It was on fire, the whole closet. The 19th century self, the culmi-
native self, can it really burn? It never burns.

Only, the ones I love die.

        ✦   ✦   ✦

He lay there dead with his eyes wide open.
*I'm supposed to say I saw that I screwed up. But all I see
are flames.*
Is that him dead or is that me?

        ✦   ✦   ✦

Why should you want or get form or content?
Some sort of social contract that no woman ever made?

It burned
but it was I

I was the closet
I was the witness
I was his
dead eyes.

He left me his dead eyes—lucky.

Introducing chance but if I'm aflame there can be no chance just flame.

There was a point where I thought a chance event would change it, what, my way of occurring. Chance can only affect women within a circumscribed space. Within the smaller of the two rooms. On earth.

Because your writing isn't a translation. It is all you are now.

All I am is this. So all of writing is changed. Now you have to compete with this reckless change. You are furious. *She is just right here. But I can't do that.*

I'm your dead eyes.

They came for him in a fiery chariot but they will not come for me for they are men.

◆　　◆　　◆

How have they left you here?
I didn't apply for a position.
Once you are left back because you didn't, there you
are   she   said. I
don't have any she left.

The federales enter forever. Lefty announces
there is a federale
available
to store your data. You have that. Data. (Or so
all the federales say.)

2

You've never come this far before.

You feel it too? *Yes.*

I've run out of luck maybe. I shouldn't have to be alive now, in the year of our President, there was no other time. No woman should be in time. I am not a woman. I am a luckless thing.

Chance will at least permit me to speak. This once. And this once, easy.

Then who has luck? No one, the new species. How? I can now deny my name.

It's this light within rat.

I was packing up again, so when I awoke I was afraid. I had had to hide my diaphragm. (But you're too old for that.)

Why did I ever have to do anything?

Momma told me I was happy; she would cry if I wasn't. This is the way this sadness works. Of course it doesn't show up in your man speculations, though you will tell me which of my neurons are lit when I'm listening to the blues. I won't let you get your hands on them, you little shit.

She and I, no one, staring at the wall where the tree shadows change to the blood red writing we, no one, can see. Can you tell me which of my neurons light up when I see it?

We stare at it from that bed. Luck would have it. This is not that kind of inheritance. It was a lot of bad luck, which is not the same as chance. Or a lot. None of this is statistical, crying out to you through his dead eyes, as he thinks how he messed up.

It's almost a story or a poem but it's really a song because it's ripping me apart.

How can you be the new species from this old mess?

The new species, the changed writing from the core of the rat light. It's the only thing left.

It's my connection with my loving momma and daddy. No one.

No one is now the only possibility.

Do you remember how you got it? Not very well. It isn't a story unless I make it that, and that would be a lie.

Maybe *you* remember how I got it, since everything's a story to you. Maybe you should tell my story if you already know it. Why do you bother reading anything anyway?

I'm talking directly to you.

The only thing to say about it is that coming down was awful in a way that was disconnected from anything in the real. So the real isn't real, but feeling awful is. I couldn't believe I could feel so bad without feeling *about* anything.

This is what you learned from those drugs, you say.

If one thinks that way I say.

Feeling awful is physiological you say.

God I hate you, I say. Yes you can find the neurons for feeling awful. Do you think you can find the neurons for the fact I hate you?

It will depend on how actively emotional the hatred is.

I can do it so coldly you can't find it I assure you.

Yes, I know you want physical exposition. You want the physical tale that you know. I'm trying to tell you, I don't have it any more. I am a dead man's eyes. I haven't seen anything for an infinity.

◆　◆　◆

Never drive a stranger from your door
Momma
Isn't that all I've ever done?

But if a stranger is more rat light I am not doing that now.
Where is chance in this light?
If it was chance I did drugs then but was it. It just was.

Jack of die
you can hear the diamonds.

If I keep hearing them
I can be dead, just listening.

Because what I love is this song.

Would you die for it? I may. But chance is involved here. I have a
slightly better than fifty percent chance of getting better. For a while at
least. They've done the statistics.
I am no one, the new species, just like you.

⬧   ⬧   ⬧

I can barely face how much she'd lost. Suffered. Depending on
which woman. Or he, too, the dead man. Which one. But you will have
your own experience and I needn't tell you a story. You have your loss. Do
you *have* it? What should you do with it? Can the neurons be found to
light up in the constellations of your suffering?

> All of our experience
> that fiery
> so no one ever even says it
> any more. It's
> exactly what no one says.
> (song by No one)

She lay there she lay and lay there. Women weeping around her
and quiet men. Her hair is on fire no that is thought, are her neurons
burning up? She isn't thinking any more, you say. I say, she's now free to
think. All of her real *life* is on fire the particulates escaping from us and
our hold.
But she loved to live. Or do you mean she wanted to survive?
That's what you'd say—the intention of the organism.
Jack of diamonds is a hard card to hold.
I can't hold on.
Hold on.

The doctor said she'd fought hard to stay alive. He was judging from what he'd seen as she lay unconscious after the accident; he assessed the spirit of a woman he'd never seen awake. I began to cry loudly. I did this to help the others know that she was dead and now we must mourn her. I remember thinking, I have to help them get to that next place. I could hardly bear to watch them move from the edge of suffering, to suffering, though I was about to grieve too.

I couldn't bear to experience *their* grief. Was my intention to survive?

You've had this experience. What do you think?

What do I do with the loss I *have*? you ask. Now that I have survived, I *have* this. In the no one species it becomes all of fire.

The intention of the organism is to know.

I say I don't have enough stamina to clean all the rooms.

I say I may not have enough stamina for all this. The others will insist I have. No one can sing the blues like no one. Believing in paradise which is red like fire.

3

I never wanted to do you wrong.
You are the one I wanted least to
do that to. This must be a universe of
care, that hoot-owl moaning; please

don't mischaracterize me, I would not
want to wrong you. I never wanted
to sing this song. But now it's mine.

That was me, I was sick. No, he lay there. His eyes were two
circles of small flames.

Since the heat in my eyes is unscientific and unsound I cannot tell
you of my death, though the purpose of literature is to court her daily and
go away. It is to create an only world of chance where anything might be
said by the dead who, only, speak.

Who else is speaking? he asked.

My sister approaches the bank of snow to die in the state mental
hospital, no one. There is no official cause of death, is there? The bank
of snow, the bank of snow is rising. I will melt it with the heat from my
dead eyes.

♦   ♦   ♦

My politics aren't yours I say
But I am yours he says. *You are.*
I would not go to war, I say,
for you, with you, anywhere.
But I am yours he says. *You are.*

There is no official cause of death, is there?
That's because we're really no one.

By chance they didn't know the cause of her death, because she
was poor. So her madness was the cause of her death. She entered the

building where she died. Causality. Nothing of her turned out well. Nothing of her turned out well. Except for the fire that left her, to merge with the fire we all are.

The light in your body is not greater than mine.

I ain't lookin' for nothin' in anyone's eyes. *So you say.*

What was good about it? Something must have been good.

But you were a man.

I got no more than you.

True.

More or less loss?

I've lost my measure for that.

I didn't care much what happened to me, so chance didn't matter. Yet some instances of chance have so scored me, I don't know if they're beautiful or plain.

If no one and I speak in the fire we can turn our backs on leaders, and all but that which concerns us, our loss.

Is it beautiful?

I always imply yes.

Where is the implication?

On the edge where I can't see, on the periphery.

♦   ♦   ♦

She falls asleep
I let go of the balloon
with her name on it.

You have nothing to hold on to.

Then how can you keep reading; but you can't stop.

These crimson flowers have gold encrustations in their centers and at their edges black rubies I recognize as menstrual blood burning. It was a sanitary pad burning in a fire, this never happened. What did?

If I were the woman who died in the asylum, and nothing of me turned out well, when she let go of the balloon of my name I didn't really die either. Like my brother's eyes later mine were fire.

My eyes were on fire of no one. They had erased me, mostly, with the lobotomy.

I'm not telling her story, she doesn't have one.

I am her.

How?

Somewhere in the genetic code you invented so precisely. For she and I are relations.

I rode the top of the train stretched out, that is my body in the tunnel. Before he died he could only think of his sister.

Brother and sister, your connections are precise because. Do you know why? There's a woman by the river is enough of the story.

She stood by the river for twenty-one years then crossed it. She had to cross it by herself.

That isn't by chance, that's what we do. It was always my intention to know that this was what I was doing. That has been my only intention.

You are all my sisters and brothers, though you might prefer I didn't say that. It is the most disruptive thing that one can say.

Having not been welcomed to safety even though she was poor and unwell, my name is no one. I never had a lover.

Why should there have been anything to do in life?

I am tortured by my heart which they say is my mind. I don't care about those two words.

I was sitting on the grass watching.

This is a check for you.

I can't buy much in the hospital, but you're my brother and gave it to me, so I like it.

I have no mind.

It hurt me too much.

They said I tried to hurt someone.

You had a genetic defect.

You are my brother aren't you defective too?

I'm not the one
I can't be the one
who.

           ◆   ◆   ◆

To give her up
to the coat
Gave her up
to her defect

no word in her throat

Your genes are defective my love

Whose mind are you? All of those I say. No one and my defect
tells you nothing. When your baby's on the cooling board. Yes I've seen
that too.

You aren't telling me anything.

The wind blew that way because it liked to.

No one will tell me where they've gone.

My Latin teacher says, those happy people are shits. They are
using an affect to tease you. We know a different language, for when the
mind breaks. Or the oldest explanation of the failure to love her.

'I knew you were in charge of me but my mind broke on its own.'

My mind is rubbed raw. The people who are in charge of me
are happy.

4

You find the needle repellent. He found it dramatically ambivalent. For me it had no qualities.

For me, I myself have hardly any characteristics.

I sometimes have them in my dreams. The story is false. Why is the story generated? For beauty's sake? For the sake of making a thing besides fire and light?

I need to gauge how much these people suffered. The body of the famine takes a deformed and ambient dream shape; and she slept in her beauty, crushed by quake and bomb.

What is a needle in the St. James Hotel next to the fact that someone never grew through all her born days? Never spoke. For thirty years like an infant. We shared genetic material.

I played for her on the piano a certain tune over and over.

This world is too full of hate. I didn't hate anyone when I used the needle, not even you. I began to hate you later, when I knew you'd always be there, holding power.

There are different hospitals to suffer in in different ways. There are healers there too.

The holder of human power has not valued the beings in these rooms as much as his bombs, his pretence of piety, and ability to seize resources. Impose his product. A murder mystery. But this is the murder. Is he of value?

> I played the song for
> you, because you
> wanted me to, though
> you could never say so.
> Who is of value? You.

> Who crossed the river
> controlled and confined
> a slave to the prevalent
> definition of defect.

I don't want there to be a president.

I don't care if I die undefended. Though I want to get well.

I hate every part of you allied with power.

But I'm speaking to you because you've been in those rooms where we can no longer touch our lovers, because their skin hurts, or touch them with words they can answer. Why do you want to do anything but understand *them*?

> Under my dress
> under my dress
> is a layer of shit
>
> Under that layer of shit
> am I
> am I.

Aren't I defective? The wind is disturbing my heart. I am the new species, born of the needle. Or. Whatever I might say. Everyone in the new species is defective.

Everyone's composed of their losses, they are purely negative, where the firing squad has nothing to aim at.

◆   ◆   ◆

A human killed by a human. Is it beautiful? Falls asleep. Disemboweled or hatcheted. Gone. Are you gone? He laid him down. I wish I didn't know you.

> I hope the steeple topples
> I hope all your religions die
> Not you, not you.
>
> The vending machine has lit up
> to tell us it's empty.
> What did you think you ever had to sell me?

You are trying to sell me
a human killed by a human.

It's been so long since I've accepted
anything you've had to tell me
that the universe has disappeared
I guess it wasn't there.

Basically I think you're no good, but I'll talk to you. I can't think
of anything else to do.

I've forgotten what I care about. The universe has disappeared
into a machete wound. Newspaper receives prizes. 'I work for my living.'
I don't. Who wants me to live?

There were those for whom few people had that wish, that
they live.

I'm no one there's no universe, he says dead.

Maybe it's all just a mood. Neurons light up in the shape. The
president's neurons and yours and mine connecting to the gaping heart
wound the machete blade has forced, sing out to the stranger, gone. Are
you gone?

On the corner of Electric and Resource.

Different language for when the mind breaks. The language
doesn't break at all, the mind does, I do, do you?

Anything I can't say
Because I wasn't supposed to
Has disappeared anyway.

What's left. The fire. What's left?
I was still letting him drive in a dream.
You don't know. I want you to know. Why?
Poor girl, dressed in black, po-lice at your back. But of course he
sang Poor boy. Because he was driving.

I am neither girl nor boy. Nor both. When I look at you you're
empty too.

If living is a defect, still it was too dark to see it. Because we had to have eyes, unless we were singers, blinded by machetes from the African future, to which we were connected. At that time I sang, Jack of die.

There is a diamond in my wound and I can't see it. In my defect. In my defect.

5

The intention of the organism is to know its life. Is that right? says the dead man.

> Your eyes are like times
> your eyes are like people
> your eyes are like failures to see
>
> my eyes are like rhymes
> my mother's back yard
> covered with pine needles
> stabbing your eyes
>
> on the ground it's misty night.
> The fence is silver-sharp spikes
>
> on the edge where I can't see
> on the periphery.

By chance I was born to appear to you to be a woman, my mother's daughter, she hears me small girl calling to her in trouble on the phone in her dream, dressed up like a choir. I forgot to tell her I was everyone. If she loves me it isn't because of the intention of the organism. It is because of the love, if you are in it you know. Then at that time that's what you know. Then in that time you don't have to know. That's why I'm not telling a story.

You don't have to solve the murder. You did it. You sold everyone a human killed by a human.

Bent over backwards, because the X-rayed beloved has dust on it. It's such a dusty rat.

I lie here his eyes dry flames and the sisters of luck.

It was my luck to be tormented by the people advancing themselves over others. It was your luck. Whose luck was it? This is going

nowhere. Because I'm dead or because it's the human situation you say
I can't see.

There's no such thing as a situation.

What about your illness? you say. Oh, the plot.

And now he is leaving and going away. Part of the murder of
my love.

It's somewhere in a torndown house that's now the post-office.
She shook it and broke it.

It's below the house that isn't there.

No one but he's someone to me, and if only these relations
remain, after all I've done and known, why did I? No one and I'm no one
to myself. Not his daughter, but I'm his daughter, because I'm him and
this love the fire that never dissolves in these eyes you've named, because
you weren't a woman. Well neither am I. And there's nothing for you, too.

If everybody's my parents and children, my sisters and brothers.
If everyone's my love. Still I saw you dead, watching over you. You were
your own angel.

> And his double instructed him
> To leave me coded messages
> From his death
> In every poem he wrote.

> This is the circumstance of trees
> Gone forever from the yard.
> It's too dark for my sister to go out.
> Don't let her go out there yet.

If you only care for others you'll get nothing in this world.
Nothing for you, too.

I cared for others all my life, he said. And still I was wrong.

I'm trying to give you everything I have. But I can't find it; I can't
find it yet.

$\bullet \qquad \bullet \qquad \bullet$

And I traded my face for one
pierced with ruby studs.
Because I loved you

I mean, because you loved me.

This is where the writing was never generous.
Where it broke into partiality
I became partial to myself. And you, to you.

◆　　◆　　◆

He wasn't right in the head. I may not be right. He checked
the door for you at night. He asked for a little money in return so you
paid him.
    Why do you think it needs checking?
    I think my property keeps me from living on the street.
    The store's gone dilapidated. We are all sorrowful because it was
us but it isn't the store now, it's empty.
    He rode a freight into town and decided to stay. He slept in
a garage.
    I'm checking the doors of your stores.

I want to break in
to say I'm leaving
I'm going to leave on
a train; I leave and
leave in the night.

No one wants to rent the store now, it's like a broken thing. My
self, he says, dead there.
    I was first pierced by love when I was born. My face and body
pierced by blues, by reds and blues, like a tribal possession.
    Sapphires and rubies of rigid pains, love bade me contort myself.
Did love itself?

It is a realer word than physiology. Though I run from it. If it got me again I could not, like this world, stand long, for I'd be too full of love, not, like this world, full of hate.

He said he had a piece of paper to prove he wasn't crazy. He said, do you?

Is it a piece of paper?

Yes, it isn't the chemicals; it's the piece of paper with the words.

When he died, Daddy raised the money for the burial. No one in such a small town should have a pauper's grave.

No one wants to rent my store now. No one wants to check the door.

I'm just like him I'm watching your stores at night. They're full of songs you don't remember.

It's an accident that I have this property where I sleep, I say. I got it through love without asking. I didn't do anything for it; I loved someone who died. I didn't even buy it myself.

Don't you cry, said his sister, don't you never cry.

◆　　◆　　◆

You are the murderer.

I always knew the house was on fire. It was one of the first things I knew.

It's still on fire, the closet. Is there anything in it?

I knew his songs before I knew his name. Everyone knows the songs before they know of the writer or singer.

Maybe your daddy sang them to you, she said.

And the one who wasn't right in the head sang Goodnight Irene, the one who, like me, was not a man or a woman, or anything.

No one would let him be a man. But I couldn't handle it, a sex like that. It's repulsive to be given a sex, when you're a being on a freight train flying by, mindless and not right.

I had slept wherever the freight train took me, he said.

I didn't have to be right in the head if I could just make it through my time.

You're right in your head.
Not if I'm him. And there's nothing to be right about.

◆　　◆　　◆

My eyes so full I could not see, is all I want.

> What's in the closet of fire
> What's that burning on your cheek
> Only a ruby where your name is.

So he wasn't loving anyone? Each minute each flame that's what
I am.

The birds sang about the murder.

They were the sapphires leaving and going away, while someone
stayed on with a mind to get through it.

The leaves were emeralds and the sun was the diamond this time.

Only in your mind, if you kept it safe.

I'm afraid that my mind isn't safe.

I'm afraid that I'm not safe.

Unless I was safe before I was born to be guarding your store.

The store lies empty, am I?

There's nothing in it but songs.

6

Have I gone beyond the periphery?

Second-hand
lingerie
bought in the night
is thin

The hardware store
opens early
full of
heavy men

beyond the periphery
where many martyrs
fell

How far gone
into my defect am I?

♦   ♦   ♦

Out on the periphery, of his eyes of red, it begins. I have nowhere to go now. I can't find it.

Go to the hardware store, where you can get something to fix something.

No go into the empty store, our store.

Here are the pieces of some martyr, to pick up and put in the store. To add to the empty store, to the store. And she's from another culture, I don't know her any more.

I never knew her.

Or myself.

Sometimes my song exists to obliterate yours; your book is

terrible, violent and long, none of the women. None of the women what? Why should I bother?

In the mind-body problem there's nothing but words. Kept in a box, with a jeweled label, of semi-precious gems.

She's just gone with the man. That's what they do, they go *with*.

What did you do in your songs?

I picked up the pieces of Osiris. But I'm not Isis.

This is so silly, ten thousand years. Of this imposed femaleness.

Pick up the martyr's pieces and put them in her box.

She was a martyr to the mind-body problem, never relinquished, always defined.

How can there be a mind-body problem, if I blow myself up in Palestine?

Put them in the box with the glittering label PROBABLE. You think this is probably all of her. You are a philosophical materialist you say.

What did you do in your songs?

I don't know, I'll never know, you say. Someone else will write them about me, won't they?

I looked into a void of love. And I fell down. There was nothing else there. No where, where I was no one.

But I have to sing this song. I'm still here.

In the hardware store you say I can find a cure. No one will be a stranger but me. A girl.

Daddy you knew.
It hurt me too much
to tell you.

What's the point of saying who anyone is or what they did they didn't do anything.

Don't learn anything from anyone. They'll tell you about the mind-body problem, or refer you to a man in the wind. The old words blow back again, all about men.

I'm dropping all of these pieces into the fire.

> I've dreamed since I was
> four years old
>
> I've dreamed since I was
> four years old
>
> that the house is slowly on fire
> that the house is slowly on fire
>
> and I can't get you to leave it
> and I can't get you to leave it
>
> and I can't leave without you
> and I can't leave without you.

You might say I was forewarned, any way. Who forewarned me?

◆   ◆   ◆

> Is there a new song in the new
> the new species?
>
> If you care. If you.

I'm so afraid in the new of the St. James Hotel. The Jamie Infirmary.

He worried about a woman in the rain. She was an image in trouble. Remembering he'd ask, Mom, Jamie in the rain?

There aren't any episodes, everything floats between everyone. No one.

He seemed secretive but he hid nothing. He was thoughtful and thought by himself. From an early age.

They were brothers.

There's nothing to hide. All stories of deception are empty.

Why don't you use more aggressive, active verbs?

I'm too sick.

From an early age we are sisters and brothers, but we think we know the numbers of us.

Hard is the fortune of all womankind.

Bought in the night for a song.

You think you won't enter the St. James Infirmary.

> How far gone
> into my defect
> am I?

> Have I gone beyond
> all the federales?

If you don't know the song, you don't know anything.

7

The song is compassion, a little girl that you think has misbehaved.

She's the one who shows me affection.

She was bad, you say.

You were jealous that she was even there. You wanted her to be hard, too, so you could punish her. But she was only thoughtful of you, small with bright hair.

All you had to do was—but you didn't. All you ever had to do.

The certainty that she
was trying to help me.
Only she could
because only a child

can.
No only a mother can.
No only a child.
A woman. A man. No only.

Goodnight Irene, the goddess of peace. Jump into the river and drown.

Don't lie to me like all the others. Don't you dare say you're the goddess of compassion.

I slept in the pines all night as I often do now.

Sometimes a girl with bright hair comes to help me, by being near. She seems to know more than I do; she seems to know.

Once she was crying when I had to go out. Everyone outside said I shouldn't show my change. Which was in my pocket.

Pine needles all over the yard, because it was late.

Don't lose your because, everyone said. Don't destroy time because then we can't have evolution. We can't have the mind-body problem. We can't have compassion.

But I am losing my because. In the pines.

In chance, in fortune, in luck, there is no because.

Once I had, and now I don't.

In love there is no because.

And I saw that when I'd used that old pine needle, I'd cast a because all over my life, and yet I passed thirty-three years without knowing my lot.

What was I doing all that time?

What have we been doing?

We've made suffering evolve. The human specialty.

I remain the girl who loves you. To get to that point I was born. You immediately said that I'd done something wrong, she said.

> The hard card to please
> has evolved.
> No, only the king
> in the black waistcoat
> has evolved.

I'm the new species, the girl says.

I want to punish you, you say.

Your parents don't like me, because I am poor. Come sit down beside me. That's all you ever have to do.

The needles can be made beautiful, if the song so chooses.

There is no choice. I'm afraid they are beautiful.

As I say, I'm afraid. I'm always afraid now, like my brother.

The river is wide, that I'm swimming with my sister.

We found our way back to shore again; we swam back to shore. The river is high and muddy, brown.

Don't take your love to town. Don't show everyone your change. Don't have a child too soon, so there can be another loving girl.

How am I changing the writing? Don't show, don't show your change.

The novel can only be motionless now. The good can only be

motionless. There are no patterns, no designs for your sufferance, if you must lose it now.

So, can I?

◆　　◆　　◆

Your self-identification
of the night. Why are
we doing
this, any of it?

Your self-identification
of the night,
in order to
be hard enough

be hard enough.
In order to
make the night hard
enough.

I almost admire the symmetries of your biological story. A body detected without sadness. By a body. Or a mind. Who cares which?

Tell me, eyes, what to do.

I believe that singing, the dead man said.

Better get all your love.

Why?

My sister went out there too soon.

Anyone did.

Tell me, eyes, what to do.

I am not a story, the eyes say.

Can't stand long, I'm already gone. The genome is an awkward song. Imposing your will on a possible future, bent over backwards towards you, only you. Bent over backwards quoting your own bible, yours.

He was dead and entered the house; he shouted, it's your self-identification of the night!

How abused were you?

I picked up a needle to measure it. Someone had said that I might, he said. He was a younger man.

In the dirty house, but what is dirt? If you're dead, it's that.

He comes back because you're afraid. You're afraid that his meaning for you is yours and not his. You're afraid that the only meaning you find is yours.

I don't have a meaning. That pleases me.

I'm the new species. Though I'm old now. Since I was your sister for forever, I mean daughter.

A stranger took me into his room and invaded me, said he who was not my relation.

I guess I never told, he said. That isn't why I come back to you. I come back to you because you think. But I don't invade you.

You country.

I knew you from the time you were a child. Are you still a child somehow? Not, I guess, if you can shout, "your self-identification of the night."

I heard that hoot-owl moaning, but I've never heard that.

My defect, he says, is so beautiful now it is all that I am.

When we die we enter our defect all together. My defect. Our defect. Who cares about evolution when there is our defect?

The closet's on fire to burn up the clothes and shoes.

8

> Sick again.
> Who's here?
> This is your defect
> it might as well be
> a diamond.

He drew the death card; I thought it was something to say about him. But it was her accident to come. I wasn't even thinking of her at that moment. Though I had all along a feeling of dread.

If you think that way.

It sticks in the throat.

It sticks; no neurons.

As a card has turned up for me. It's better to call it this. Cards.

Years later I showed him his card. Accidentally. He said it was his illness, the ten of swords. Was it my fault? His angel says no.

This is a better system: one looks into the blazing defect, all at once. Not really such a hard card to play.

But I never want to turn a card over again.

> Don't turn that card over.
> Momma, don't
> look at it yet.

> Maybe you won't ever
> have to look at it.

He was afraid of magic, because it was there.

But it's just a scientific cause and effect.

I took a card back there, I say. I chose a card face down.

Sometimes I've seen the future.

Do you have to?

I saw the blazing love there is, but I'm afraid of that. Even of that.

If my mind should break, would it just be broken that's all.

I was afraid, for awhile, that I might kill someone. Everyone does, at a distance. But I never killed anyone, though that was only personally.

> Killing
> for all my born days,
> across the water
>
> and in the death chambers
> of the hearts
> you chose
> to stop.

No one's heart is like mine.

Hearts are all the same and can be pierced, torn out, eaten. We the victors feed on your heart.

Why not? Why not eat it if you've killed him?

♦   ♦   ♦

There isn't any way to be.

I will meet you where you've gone. The cards are blank; the cards are empty there.

If I can just have one last cut.

Do you have a plan for the new?

The cards be blank. The symbols be over.

I will tell my fortune with the blank cards of blank.

What do you see?

These cards are old. That's how they know you.

If you don't have anything, they can fill you.

He said his mother knew the cards. He said they scared him.

I don't want to do the cards anymore.

What do you see?

I see that I will pass something on to the folk. If it's sad could I have helped that? It was passed on to me.

The new species is in me, this moment the card is blank. It shines. The War Memorial's gold and has no names on it.

This moment the card's bright blank. I'm turning it up for you. Me. No one.

Someone showed her the cards, then she knew them.

You showed me a card
I forgot
You showed me again
It was mine.

It stretched forwards and bent backwards, it was a symbol that knew everything.

I don't believe in the cards.

I don't believe in anything.

They say I'm not worthy of entering your door. Your door is empty and full of light.

She was a rose and a flower. I think she was cast away. An older woman took charge of her and taught her about the cards. She had borne a fine son. I haven't seen them in years.

Make me a pallet down soft and low. I once heard an old woman say, I only need a pallet to sleep on.

If the cards are operative, why bother with any more? Than a pallet and cards.

I seem to come from another time. I might be an image on a card. Because I'm surely no one now, Momma.

The high priestess he said, as I handed him his cane he'd dropped.

You have left the world of the mind-body problem and entered the world of symbols. You're just there. One or two others might be along this time.

But I don't want to enter that world again.

I'm going down Laredo
I'm gonna tell my fortune

with the blank
cards of blank.

You're going to have to face that love.
I can't stand to.
The high priestess for that moment is no one.

9

I'm afraid you'll tell me he wasn't like that, he was like *that*.

You don't know my fortune. His fortune.

If you were to read me I'd just die. But I know I can't be read. You don't have the right to read my pain, he said. You can't help me now.

◆　　◆　　◆

I don't want anyone to suffer more than I have. This is what you can take.

Oh no, you can take more.

He couldn't even take it, I say.

Someone's trying to read me. Someone's trying to read me. There's nothing to read, but I know one thing. No I don't. Know a thing. Keep your hands off my neurons.

But I hear something.

You can hear things.
You can hear things
no one else can.

He says a creature whose hands. I'm attuned to the sounds of those flames. And. The more I hear the closer I am. To them.

I am standing in another world. Please take off your hospital gown. It isn't a gown, it's the color white. I can't ever take it off again.

Sometimes I hear it, better than see it.

Who do you know who's been there?

I have. But I forget. There may be continuity in neurons; but light passes through in jagged sheets. It hurts my hearing, then goes.

Hurts?

Because I am hurt; I mean you. But it isn't really light.

She stood in her poor house happy. It felt like it hurt. The house was a tent, and she wasn't even thinking. But you want to say that she was.

What was she doing?

She was always going on, widowed three times and never a penny.
Or that's your story part; she's just standing. Can you stand it? I ask her.
She says yes, but how can she? I think I love her, but she died the week I
was born.

I can't tell you everything I've heard. My senses never diminish.
The flames may appear to be in my eyes but my skin is forever touched.

You can't travel now.

A blackbird's song made the muscles near my eyes contract.
Outside the window. Outside or inside.

You can't travel.

It is my forehead, the word of deity, no one.

This is what you can take. I could never have found it, that way
where everything was. I passed through because I had to, but I was always
listening elsewhere. Do I need pain to hear it? Do I need this passing
through?

Answer if you can.

◆　　◆　　◆

I'm going down to Mexico after you die. I'm escaping. The
federales won't try to catch me, I'm too crazy. I always go down to
Mexico after you die, in a car with two other guys.

Do you ever know who you're talking about?

Not even when it's me. It's all the same.

I had to kill them to stay alive, he said. I was always afraid.

You're the new species though you're dead now.

The new species is what I know. We defective ones are the new.

I'm dead because I couldn't take it any more, he said.

That scares me. I'm talking directly to you.

Are you scared for me?

I'm afraid. I want to get past that, past the periphery.
I see symbols and hear songs. They concentrate the fear so I won't
have it. I don't want to *have* it. I still have it for you, even though
you're dead.

I'm where he's hurt and
I can hardly stand it.

I'm surrounded by
hard light; surmounted.

He may really want
to be extinguished

which is not the same
as dead.

I'm going down that road feeling bad. It isn't me it's you. Bad for
you; bad about you. Him.

They had to kill more people, having no right to be there. This
keeps going on everywhere, while a she stands in front of her tent-house.
That's what a she does. Never forget that dying is something you can do
without money.

They only let him go so wrong out of kindness I suppose.

I'm past the periphery of wrong, he says, it was just wrong.

Is it just wrong? I took him in anyway. I took him in anyway,
she says.

Have you ever helped create a tormented human being?

I walk very slowly now, but I do little harm, I say.

I'm not talking about him. I'm talking about being with him, in
my mind though he rejects me. He feels he doesn't deserve company.

I've got to get past the people.

I need to be with their spirits.

I'm covered with human spirits, in my pockets, in my shoes.

The spirits in this clarity
are the same old ones
everyone.

There are no arguments. I just don't know what to do with you.

I went down there to pay my fine. It wasn't the same as healing. I went to pay my fine; I went to pay my fine. Over and over. It wasn't the same as healing. That's what I want to get past.

I see you, he says. Though I don't know if I am doing it. You are an image surrounded by red. Somewhere. There is no one here to see you, but the image exists. Not in eyes. Says the man on the bed.

> The image exists
> not in eyes.

If I'm there, am I alive? If I'm that image.

Don't call my name while I'm riding this train. Don't tell no stories please don't tell no lies. Don't don't dont.

I'm turning into something I never foresaw. When I get there I'll recognize it.

You won't have to. Will you be you?

The red becomes richer. Senses are clues. Not useless. Not treetrunks to be uprooted. But they hurt so much.

10

I say the error's gone
and no cathedral
can hold this song for
me.

There's no
woman
anywhere
No edges speaking.

◆　　◆　　◆

He was sitting there. His hair glossy, he hid his face.
Where have you been?
In the country of war. I don't even want to be an image.
Your image can still be light. You are still made out of light. This
was more truly our conversation.
There was dust on the man. A conscience was dust; it came from
everywhere and was the same difference. There were too many versions.
I am simplified by my spell, he or I said.
You didn't cast it, we did, others might say. You don't do any-
thing by yourself, they might say.
What can I trust? he said.
Your death?
My death, he said. For that was right.
Mine will not be right, I say. For I won't have vindicated women.
I won't have seen the fall of male power. I won't have helped heal the
earth. Why should I die and men still hold power? Why should I have
lived to be treated like a woman?
I am an image, the goddess said. You can pray to me if you have
to but I won't answer you.
And them that don't like it can leave me alone.

The little girl is an image.
But I deny commonsense notions. That's another dream.
It isn't real unless. You're standing there.
Standing there, he injected the drug that killed him.
'I can prove there is no life, as you define it.'
And I, I had once injected a toxic drug too. To be with you.
No one.

◆   ◆   ◆

We saw you come over.
You can't come here unless you understand us. You must have heard us calling.
I'm speaking to you all the time.
Those others can hurt you so bad, because they're alive.
I hurt *them*, he said. Can you please help me?
First he had asked other people, but they hadn't seemed to understand where he needed to go or why. He himself wasn't sure.
Can you please help me? I don't know who I'm asking. The beings I can't see.
I think they finally helped him; came for him and took him at his word. *I'm suffering.* They take you in.
I'm not dying, I say. I'm doing a different thing. I'm being guided by them.

What is owed to
beauty:
finding it out
that is the ode
to beauty.

And no cathedral
can hold this song
for me.

If you see it that way.

I just see it. I'm seeing it now. I have become this. While you were still worshipping violence.

Injected the drug. Because it was an image of relief. It wasn't an image of the world.

Everything hurts inside the flames, the most beautiful rubies. For the families on relief.

Everyone robbed me, even the outlaws. Violent consciences. I say.

I've injected the drug; I'm you, too.

I'm trying to share your conscience. I'm trying to give you mine, but I can't absorb your violence. I don't have a violent conscience. You know that, and it's part of what kills you, I think.

The little girl, compassion. She should just have been a child, he said.

It's been sitting there all these years. It's my bag, it's my clothes, it's my laundry. Said a voice, for me. Said any old voice, no one.

You don't cross it by yourself. You cross it with all these others.

I want to cross the river by myself.

You can't.

This is monkey pain.
Or so all the federales say.
But I wouldn't say that.
I would say rat light.

◆   ◆   ◆

Can you please help me? But there's no one here. Myself.

Anyone says
But I know
one thing

he's gone.
                    Do I
know another
after all?

Will he or she help me? No one.

I didn't care any more how they'd reduced us to gender and race. I didn't seem to have enough time. I want to be where you are.

There's no place to rest, he said. Used to be a moment on a point. He didn't have a face like a mask.

Can you please help me?

I'm almost telling this story but I'm not going to. The old kinds of details aren't right any more.

I'm talking about beauty.

It isn't yours. You can't have it.

I'm not the one who put the edges in my eyes, am I? But I'm burning them now. To see it.

Where is the girl who helps me?

She isn't a girl or a woman. She isn't a boy or a man. She floats there where the edges fail. She has no fortune or defect.

Everybody I met
gave me no rest
but you.

I I

She was still beautiful, with a diagram on her torso, which showed how she was certified meat. She also had a rash on her face. My sister, with my own, sister symptoms.

I tried to tell her how beautiful.

You can be cut up by any man's ideas. Enacted by the blades of progress. Not beautiful; but you are. Singing from beneath the imprinted map. Embedded into your breasts. By whom?

I'm staring out the window of the St. James Hotel. It's just a hotel.

The closet's on fire. I tell someone to call the fire department. It's the department of standing long and long in the fire.

Only the old sounds help. They're all I know, if I know. He said. He was listening to the song, Cattle Call.

The yellow-gold figure detaches from my body to float before me, the goddess of compassion.

Don't you tell me no stories.

Marry again
marry again
whose eyes
can see the wind

whose eyes that can
see
another world
would marry

this one again.
I can't, he said/

she said, not
again.

I know him but I don't really. His eyes see another. Your eyes don't see me when you look.

If I share your conscience, will you share mine? Your eyes don't see me when you look.

I've done something wrong. I've done something wrong; but *you* did it. You always do it.

Who will prevail? I need to destroy your ethic, before I die. But not you.

I have that diagram on my torso, which shows how I am culpable butcher's meat. My face is broken out. I've never done anything, I don't deserve this at all.

Who will say you're still beautiful, if you're a killer? he said.

The goddess is a simple gold fire, heart of a ruby. I saw her that night in my room. But she arose out of me.

I see you though you don't see me.

I see her but she doesn't see me.

♦   ♦   ♦

I'm the ghost behind your definitions.

It was his angel double. He sat up in the hospital bed, to talk to the spirits in the room. When there was such pain in his cut-up spine; and his double sat up in his body, sat up without discomfort. To speak to the dead. And there was no mind-body problem. I witnessed this scene. But I couldn't understand what he said.

Who are the living? What about them?

Don't you know who you are? You are rat light, the angel.

And the angels laid him away.

Please don't leave me here. Again.

But I'm left.

And if I can't get along with you, with all you, what will I do now?

Saying this life is compelled. I traveled to my turbulence, for another injection, of the medicine. Treat me, needle.

I went to the doctor
to be healed

What else would a
doctor do

but heal me?

I'm not too gone to be
healed, am I?

I'm not too gone
am I?

But he couldn't be healed. If I can be, will I feel guilty? The wind,
nothing. Everyone treat me gently.

Conscience goes to spell, so I simplify. You simplify.

I'm casting a spell of protection; it might last an hour in this air.

We should know we can't stand long. A white bird flies up, from
a midnight blue sea.

If you wanted to dance, a long time ago.

There's a beauty imposes no questions, in the process of losing
edges, until the bird's eyes are clear to see. Two circular lines. You were
alarmed because you had to fly, but now you're a high-flying bird, white
light with no symptoms.

She's gone
she and the doctor
together
could not hold back

her double. But I
thought my love was
her other
aspect, he said.

We were in that outer room where one waits for word. I already knew the doctor's news would be bad.

Because you've seen them, how they fly up, behind your eyes.

I've seen so much there. The only gold. I've seen that I wear it there.

I've seen you, all my other doubles, too.

Please help me, I'm sick.

That's all right I'm here.

The yellow-gold image behind my eyes, leading me on, he said. The new species.

Part bird. Part rat. Part voice. Part elephant.

Trying to forget, but you can't do that.

12

The man on the bed shares genetic material with me. Anyone does. Particularly so does he. What is that?

> Under which
> Am I
> Am I.

The man on the cooling board doesn't share my genes in that same way. What is that? Which man? you say. Which cooling board?

What is an image? Only to be on the wind. In the mind or not. Can I be that? Does it belong to you and not me?

I think he sees me where nothing is.

Which man? Does he see?

I've broken loose from my own chest, and float, yellow-gold, above you. I would help you, no one. Fresh from my injection, I am a projection, over your self-identification of the night.

I can take you there. You can take me there.

Across?

Maybe. But there may be more than one kind of across.

Everything burning.

My image is a projection, but I don't resemble myself. I look like the goddess of compassion. Though that isn't part of my folk. But the folk's always changing.

Why does my father need me if he's dead?

Pity my seed, he says, not corruptible but hurt.

What else have I ever done?

◆　　◆　　◆

I don't know what to do, if I can't get along with you. There's no one here. Everyone's here in this moment.

I'm trying to make it the rest of the way. Beyond the periphery, where there is no genetic material, where there is nothing, nothing you say.

She's got every moment glued to her. She can break into each one, on a dollar. She was my best Momma.

I hate those moments. They're breaking my mind. Please let me go free.

My easy rider's with my sister, who's me. Back in the past in the free. No this is the free. No I'm still your image.

I've been spliced into so many ones, that I can only be a single image, no one.

I'd take pity on myself, but nothing would happen, would play; another moment whirling away. But still I'm trying, trying to take pity on myself.

Her breasts are misshapen, cover her grotesque nipples. You have so many defects how can you breathe?

It can't be that same old image of her.

> I'm leaving you
> I can't be who
> I used to.

The wind shook the rain; she'd never scream or anything. It was just a sad mojo. No one wanted it any more, do you?

Broke and ain't got no time. There must be some time. Time to get there. Click. No. He's across. We saw him stretched out on the long white table.

No he slept with my sister, last night, me.

> Defect defect
> put its arms around
> me
> make me cry
> It's a hard card to stay.

I got to get there, Daddy.

My sister has two or three shadows in her hands; left over from the conflagration. There are always more cards to play.

The congregation is calling; but I'll never go *there* again.

It's going to be all right, he said.

No it isn't, I said. As he died.

So is it?

I'll never know. Ask the man: is it all right? Why doesn't the man ever ask me?

I have a defective space between my breasts.

You can't find anything but genes. If I ask you if it's all right, you say yes but you only mean for you.

It was all supposed to help me breathe, but everything you done made breathin' worse. Everything you done made breathin' hard. Any child knows.

He can find breathing, but he can't find air.

Why do you keep calling life a defect?

What else call it if you keep trying to fix it?

I'm trying to fix your illness now, you know. Says the man. I'm trying to fix your defect.

It may be what I love now, I say.

＊　　＊　　＊

I ran toward her before, it was before my hair turned black, he said. I ran towards my mother. She was widowed three times.

You are a boy; and I am an unborn, said I.

There were many beautiful landscapes in that state, he said. My sister played the guitar, but I could sing. I had an ear for changes of pitch. I could hear those changes and make those sounds.

> You were the folk
> when you began
> any babe.

> Any
> Babe
> comes to have the ear.

She hears the changes in words alone.

I can hear everything now. Everything there is. I can be good, baby.

I think he knew songs like, So Long It's Been Good To Know You, 'cause I'd always known it.

Don't say knowed it, don't say cain't like Grandma. These gospel beads around my back are almost as pretty as thee. Some *don'ts* are pretty.

And stay all night with me. The never again. Not with my sister but me. I'm talking to my lover on the cooling board.

Which lover on which cooling board? you say.

I'll never know how to live, will you? That was blood in my eyes, not flames.

I'm the folk, no one; Daddy, that's who I am.

Momma, it hurts me too. All of you.

If this were a novel, a lover would stay all night. But all those friends I ever had are gone. And no novel's true. Not true, like you. Like you were.

I played a song while he was sick, over and over, about a rambler. Who's ever known a rambler?

All the friends I ever had are gone.

Can the image hear it? Depends on which man you ask.

There are so many ways of hearing. To be is to be like sound, isn't it light? *Which* doesn't matter. I'm talking to you. And so this gold-red rose, flat as an emblem, has left my chest empty. The space between my breasts is empty.

He's lying there leaking songs. Which man? Which bed? Which cooling board?

13

Whose tears can't I bear?

The code's not just genes but songs.

He cried after his other sister died. The code's not just genes
but tears.

I have blood or flame on me, so I can change all writing. With
a red-hued jaguar cat along. Blood in my eyes.

You have not to know, until it's done. You have not to know. No.
I want to know now.

She has a high-pitched hypnotic voice. She's with a reddish jaguar
cat. She's dyed my hair to match it.

This is a folk procedure too: whose tears are calling now?

I can hear the tribes moaning.

Placed by whom within your spine your brain your eyes, whose
tears or songs? Whose moan?

Placed within me. Can I take you across? My hair is reddish
with blood.

She has the voice of hypnos. The blood or flame in my hair and eyes.

I've gone with the jaguar in the blood-red coat through the soul-
hell transformation.

In that old dance hall, where only neurons or songs or tears float,
someone is chanting, in order to cross over.

As I had said, there must be other ways of leaving. Of returning.

This song lifts you. Way above the black coat. Way above your
self-identification of the night high golden moon, an image.

I am flying, for you're sick.

After my injection, like any folk shaman of the path.

In the beginning when young I tried and failed; and as I suffered
more and more, improved. Now in my defect I'm best of all. In my earlier
injections, I was the twin of this now. I took on the stories I am casting
away like old medicines.

The songs are inside within small red cells. The stories, once
coiled into snakes, I cut to pieces. They're trembling words which connect
vibrationally.

His tears are old. And now that they're flames I can use them. In the dissolution, of my wrong location.

From the dark blue dock of the spine. Cast off. Shook it broke it. Tears are old spine.

It's good that you're trapped in your illness.

> I'm going to find your soul
> I'm going to find your soul
>
> This is the oldest song.

✦   ✦   ✦

My old friend. Could I call it that, so fierce? A visage in the orange flash.

It eats you. Because you think that you're people.

I have a necklace of bloody teeth for this cure. Teeth of many martyrs; the stars above the barren town.

Move in waves. Crickets sing too. See the empty haunt here, it eats you.

But how many of death's teeth have I stolen? It doesn't have any left. Pass through the image of death.

He's taken your name. I had no name.

Do not remember me, unreal lord. You are wrong about everything.

> There's a cure
> in each instant
> if you can keep it
> from ending.

Don't think what the songs think now. I hear her hypnotic voice, the blood on my hair.

Soon be over. Sorrow will have an end. No don't think what the songs think. Just think how they sound.

Don't answer if you can. And he walks with me and he talks with me. Where the sister dwells, with the flame jaguar.

Is this the debt to beauty? The whole conception was bloody.

Heap of silver and turquoise. My magic.

> If you change you
> show it indifferently. Crickets
> don't change the federales' ways.
> Crickets
> don't even know the federales.

Cross the silver mesh path there.

Turn off the law.

I'm not part of your growth chart, saying this life is compelled. I have the unconditioned, in a heap in my pocket. She says in her bloody monotone.

Where is the change?

It's in you.

> It's
> my magic
> no one's.

         ◆   ◆   ◆

I'm wading in shallow water. Wade in the water. Lift your skirt. I've done this so many times.

How did you learn it?

It's in my genes. It's in my global genes.

There were once jaguars everywhere around here. There will be animals in your deaths, won't there?

I'm talking directly to you.

I'll greet my defect my soul, with this animal, part of the folk.

If I find your soul do you want it?

I see it everywhere, past the death visage.

If I find your soul do you want it? Do you even know? Do you even know what part of you you are?

◆　　◆　　◆

       Big medallion
       the gold you invested
       a precision of sorrow

       cut out to be a face
       you almost remember.

It floats within.

On the road of the souls, the jaguar and I. Through the deserts of dying words, and spirits thick as bats.

Plow on through Corolla Pass, to meet my love. See the souls around me everywhere. One of them is you.

I know who I was, says the soul. I don't try to remember it.

       It's the promised line
       Not the promised land
       What you recall
       That's all.

He has a big face; his eyes are closed. I wouldn't want to go back, he says.

I don't blame you.

What will you return with, then?

A fair deal, I say.

When I died, he says, everything was unresolved. That's always the case with deaths. There is no official cause of death, is there?

Yes, there is, but it isn't correct.

I had what you have now, he says.

That's not why I came. Or is it part? I should bring back a soul. It's my work, after all.

Shades crowding round the bloody jaguar; shades crowding
round my blood-red hair.
Then I see her. Young, eyes closed.

> I see my
> own soul.
>
> How do you know?
>
> It stands between
> the king and queen
> of swords.

There are no rooms here. There are no beds. Where is there rest?
I ask.
That's not the right language, he says. There's plenty of rest here.
As I once told you there'd be.
She's resting, you know. She needed some peace, he says.

> I see my
> own soul there
> heavily guarded
>
> by others.
> As always.

This is an ancient procedure. I know that she doesn't want to die.
Though her land is condemned. My own soul doesn't want to die.
The hoot owl sings; the jaguar grins.
I'm taking her back, I say. And I reach for her hand and lead her
from between the king and queen.
Then I face my old love, no one.
I gave you the illness, he says.
It doesn't matter, love, I say, leaving.

14

My childhood was held on my own, beyond any wheel.

Somewhere like ancient Assyria. How near Assyria is!

I waded in the shallows. I never wore shoes on the road. Over the fields, where I breathed.

This is a heavenly tree. And the world is open windows. Who needs angels? If they speak, I'm not even going to listen.

How near the ancient culture is! I see the carved foundation, at the foot of the green hill. Designs in stone.

Has anybody seen my love? Oh, I don't care.

This is the morning of the age I was, six, when she died in the state mental hospital. There was never an official cause of death for her.

If I've brought back my soul, have I brought back hers too, even if she couldn't leave?

Have I brought back yours too?

She and I are both innocent in the photo, the man says. The man on the bed says.

Anyone's transparence, I want you to be here with mine. I'll keep it with mine.

My purpose is to return with your soul. The last fair deal, for you were fair.

✦   ✦   ✦

I ride the exactitudes of pitch, the tune, in words alone. I wouldn't be able to take the journey, if I couldn't hear the poem.

Could you voyage without the register of changes?

Who do you serve? Do you serve somebody?

I serve the poem, no one.

As they are taking down the tent, as if there were no more poetry. See the ghosts of it; woman chanting, blind man sings. Like no one. This land, condemned, endures. I could never be ashamed of my life.

Hearing that old owl sing.

I was born to be your poet. I am the woman, your poet. All that I am.

And I know one thing. No one. Is the poet. I am.

She just did what she had to do.

Who else can do this? No one. Any no one who cares to, and the eyes above, where I have been, approve.

I don't think you had a choice except to be a poet, he said. But this world still can't stand long. He was already sick.

There's an enormous pine beneath which she lies. Momma, in the pines and of all the pines, this one above, with some of its needles gone yellow, is the most beautiful.

It can't stand long, can it? More and more parts of us die, covered up after, by the long black coat of his preference, ignorance.

I prefer the live versions. The performance of the search for the soul.

> The scratches in this
> recording
> are due to a perfect technique,
>
> beauty's intransigence.
> Them that don't like it
> can leave me alone.

Take care of the pines where we sleep.

I never do anything else.

The photos of the dead women, too, were faint and silvery, scratched. I knew who they were, my relations, and I still longed to help them. Though they were dead and I would become one of them.

> Never got what we should have had
> Never got what you should
> Equality is a poor word
> For life.

You can't have what they had, their loss.

Or else the rich would live and the poor would die.

She don't have no where to go, wandering round from door to door.

She's travelin' through the land. Don't you hear me calling?

I remember when Momma dreamed of her crying outside her bedroom window, trying to get in. She was, at that time, far away, in the hospital for the defective. She for whom I had often played a song.

Don't you lie to me. Tell me where did you sleep last night.

She couldn't lie. She never grew, never spoke.

Beneath the great pine tree, I think all this, in my high old bed, Momma said.

I do whatever you do.

Momma, I keep trying to find her soul.

But she has it. Don't you know?

◆   ◆   ◆

In the boughs where the shamans come to life. Boughs where the poems' dark eyes hang.

It's such an old function I've forgotten everything that I know.

Except how to do it again.

He still knew how as he lay, mostly blind, dying. He just didn't do it anymore. He was it.

Kiss him goodbye in the hospital for the moneyless. There's another poet, lying over in another ward.

Which one? Which poet? Do you know him?

I know one thing, nobody can sing the blues like Blind Willie McTell.

I am your poet, Momma said. I gave you everything I had. Though you thought I was wrong sometimes.

I didn't give you genes, I gave you poems.

It's all the same being, wrapped up.

Beneath the tree on the river bank. Wrapped up with Black Jack Davy.

Divided, spreading their wings
they fly up from the tree.

Though tonight they'll lie on the
cold cold ground in his arms.

I gave you everything you know.

This world tree is patterned but unconditioned; because you never know. If you'll make it or not to the heavens and bring back your soul in this song.

There's no because.

Who do you serve?

The tree, she said. The tree with golden needles, never barren.

But nobody could sing the blues like you could. Singing his/her/ your song, all wrapped up one. In the arms of the old infirmary.

I'm gazing out the window, all the windows.

Everything's in motion, he said. At least that's all that I see. I only see movement now.

I'm its audience. He may have said. Still interested, though he hadn't walked for months.

◆   ◆   ◆

If I'm not your poet, who is?
If you don't want a poet
    then don't say so.
Baby, please don't go.

I gave up my long blue gloves and shoes of finest leather. But I never left my babies. I bore them in the great pine tree and we lived there together. In the tree of shamans. We still do.

Don't lie to me. Who are you? Just who are you?

I am the poet.

Made the words around him ring. How old are you my pretty little miss, a long time ago and now.

You never will want for money, because you never will want it. What will you forsake?

I'll forsake everything but the tree. The pilgrims call it the tree of life.

THE BLACK TRAILOR

THE BLACK TRAILOR (A NOIR FICTION)

I never saw you lining the all black trailor. It was a beautiful hit. If I find you again, after, where there are no trails? So you never can tell. Watch it.

That sunlight tweaking you's just light. Everything is. So what did you have to gain?

I'm always looking for you, because that's clear. The heat's reflected in my eyes, back in the past or out in the future. I've got no one else to tell. Am I a beggar, in receipt of nothing yet?

It was a great emptiness. Wasn't it full of the figures of love? Only physics? But there are many kinds of physics. There is the kind, for example, where words move objects constantly.

And then there's the humming within me, that's here.

It might have to be sung again and then again.

But I don't want you to sing it. I don't like your breath.

The hit in the future came down in the future, I tell you. That might be now.

I don't believe in intercession or in the wheel. Though one of my names might be Catherine. Little known, if anyone.

The violence we read about goes down. To trace some kinds I've known, I'd have to violate telling; because violence doesn't always proceed directly from body to body. It flows from the heart to as far as the heart can't see. You will never believe you've done it, done something to me.

> His ghost arms closing
> round me from behind;
> Try to break their power
> Try to rip the beads of power
> from his neck
> I can't see his face. I don't
> even know who he is.
> And the freedom I
> have, I don't have in this hour.

In my dream I pull at the amber beads as he holds me from behind; I hit at him in that awkwardness. He won't let go.

I may be addressing him, you who'll sing as if you suffered.

We brought violence to us and loved it, in our songs and stories. We love it more than anything now. The hit in the black trailor though, that's my death.

Before that, I want to send thoughts, as unstruggling patterns, not lines of words. Maybe to the weather, forced into its own new violence. We've created it and now are its martyrs; it comes, greeting any saint with new flame, any bird or flower, like a blinded thing.

I talk, or think, to everything, am I trying to surround it? I'm afraid my body won't fight for me against the dark. See, I'm always using the language of combat: it's so deep in. I think you want me to fear you.

I don't know if you are a man or a far-ranging mood. Wide over, break that particular physics.

I personify my eyes, which cannot see by themselves. To you I personify my heart or sex; I don't want you happening to me. This is worse than any crime, or a story with people you think you can see.

I saw one dark wing, no wren. That is the dark wing and it is actually me; for I saw it had my she-head. That was what I could see. That is my being.

And after that the ships on stage had toppled. They fell over like cardboard ghosts, darklit.

(2)

The ocean floor observed inside love is empty, stripped of its life. We've killed it. So, is the ocean still within love? Another martyr. It is supposedly without a wish—which is a word in a language, or a physical—of physics—force; the physics of the psyche. See these Greek words? They don't mean anything, do they? If one is the ocean.

Wanting no forces to exist outside of us, you are living the story of a murder. You are running from yourself, thrilled, and blinded. You don't want to hear; you believe in the cop and the lowlife. On the ocean bottom. For you, it might as well be dead.

It's a trembling crumbling lightning order. Green. I know the words shouldn't be in any order, but I'm obliged by the language to keep them in line: trembling, crumbling, lightning. Why isn't "lightning" "lightening"?

I must change, lying on a dead shoulder. The shoulder decomposing, green and alive in decay. It might be the shoulder of myself or a lover, the hill far away. I'm rugged enough, I say, for this.

The looters tap at my breastbone and pull out the connections. Then they take my freedom, their bloody food. But it's you I'm talking to.

Are you corruptible? I say. Like this body whose head has come off, in the world of no souls to matter. You are corrupt, I say; you believe in death.

I'm talking to you, I say. Your gun can kill the whole hill. You'd kill anything, you. The body sat there because you wanted to see it. With its putrefied tattoo that you love, in the titillation of the dirge.

If the ocean is empty so am I. I'll have no more dreams. The dirge presents a full complement of chromosomes, disinfected.

Maybe it was a suicide, in order not to go through more time. Maybe you think the world is tired of its time, committing suicide on its own. You say, do you always talk about it as if it were one thing? I say, I talk *to* it as if it were one thing.

You enter the lives of people who don't exist. You want some of them to die in the course of the story. The face is blown away, the fingerprints are decaying.

But first two people become lovers. I now watch them make love. He is both a man and a literary character. In her own room she keeps her artist's things, though she's fictional too. Enclosed in a circle I watch her with sadness; will I never be that person again? My fingerprints are almost gone from that scene.

It's a beautiful hit if your identity is the story. Are you identifying with death, in anticipation because death's you? But it isn't necessarily me, I say; so I may look for you later. I will confront you somewhere where you aren't the order, aren't in order, I say to you.

She is Catherine, a martyr who never lived. They will have no evidence of her existence. She will be robbed of her sanctity. They won't be alive at the same time as she, trembling crumbling lightning. I don't know if it's lightning or lightening.

His name is Mark; it will stay in place. For that really is the past when I was broken. When only a Mark would do fine.

I said, I like this play. You said, it's no good. You placed the corpse onstage, and it became the good. Was it mine? If I am, say, the ocean; the earth; whatever dies for you.

I will search for you after your death, to confront you. I will pose to you your timelessness and lack of fixity. I will say you have now never won.

I will search for you across heaven, for you marked me when I was indistinct, when I was loving, I say. When the drama still had its humor, and the ocean was unjudged by you. Before you thought it worth destroying like the sky the earth, in what order name those three spiraling? When I didn't have to be either a woman or a bird. When the bloody wheel wasn't tattooed into decaying flesh. When we didn't love the murder.

I will search for you across light to undo the murder. How can I let go, I say, just because there's no time now?

(3)

And now that you're dead in the future.

Has anybody seen the corpse of the county? country? heart? What order for those three spiraling? I can step out of any dark or light reach now and face you.

The river has receded; the water's dried up; what's left is you, only you. You were always the only one for you. Someone might say I should kill you, now that you're dead, but who's dead here?

Can the dead kill the dead?

Keep going back, keep going forward; but there's void either way. Orange streak sky. I always remember both ways, what's gone from the earth as I beg for it back from who? There's only us.

And somehow the corpse is here too, where we're nowhere. In fact it's all you care about. You need to get rid of it, don't you? Move it, you say, move the whole corpse of earth away.

Move the whole planet somewhere?

You say that you're dead and it's dead: can't it be pushed back through a hole in timelessness?

You say that I can't really get at you.

You're not where you expected to be dead, I say.

Is this a system? you say.

If you trusted yourself, I say, there's nothing here to trust. If you trusted what they told you back there, well as you can see . . . no heaven/hell, no bardo/rebirth, no extinction.

I can follow you for all eternity. It's easier without the trail, the line. No borders. There may be no borders between us; have you noticed that?

I have an icy wind for a mind, and you've never had your own mind. The world your letter to me, as in the agreed on version, destroyed by infant preachers. You.

And you run, and I follow. Inside you, so you know. How long does this last? you ask—is it an in-and-out dream, that I'm a bloodhound, though we're both bloodless?

> You thought you were a man
> You thought when you died you'd be a
> dead man. Can someone explain my
> condition? you say.
> But I don't want *you* to explain it,
> you say.

I'm injecting you with sadness, the deadliest syringe. Is it a murder? Is this your story? But you have no character to serve it; and I only talk like a blighted land. What do you feel now, I say?

You say you didn't know that sorrow was everywhere.

Why shouldn't it be? And now, you're always part.

I want you to know
I want you to know
you'll never escape me.

You say it courses through you, you say it's all you know, and I
am cold—icy—to give you my sadness. All through you. And there is no
other god.

It pulsates then collapses into a gesture—a sigh; it's vast and local.
Why can't it be torn or burned? you say. Doesn't one pass through it.

When time exists, I say. Now that there are no borders, it's
all yours.

Everything was green and it's over. Those white lilies must have
loved you, rottening to brown, as the snow on the mountains recedes.
Don't remember your love, it'll just make you crazy that way.

Why isn't my love here? you say.

(4)

You have never had a plan except to use love for yourself, forget-
ting it during the day. Because there was so much to do; destroying me
with your control, which was illusory. Since you served another power,
not supernatural at all. Just another power, and who cares which
one now?

As for the body. As you called it. You tried to disfigure it in all
ways; to make sure nothing else was there. The cut flesh, the excised eyes,
the organs tumbling out.

You saw what you wanted to. But your wanting wasn't your own;
you weren't ever in charge of your own wish, I say. You say that you
didn't wish for anyone to die.

But you didn't wish that one didn't. Never knew where your
orders came from. You didn't even want to know. As long as the details
of the day or the page had been marked for you. So there could be the
world. All you needed were names, in order to go on; more names
and things.

You say that you didn't kill him.

Him? I say.

All you needed were more words, I say. To invent what people say to each other. What they must say to each other. Why are you afraid of that corpse?

You're not afraid of it, you say that you've proved that by cutting it up in so many ways—no you didn't do that, you say.

I say, I let you kill me, because I knew I wouldn't die. I'm the one you kill, every time. This is how our lives have been arranged: I die and come back, I say. You're frightened by the lack of specificity here. Though you'd say there's no argument, if there's nothing to hold on to. But, there's nothing to hold on to. What can you say?

You insist on existence as you've described it, you say. You say that this is or isn't existence; but all that was real, before, was so because of its detail.

Why do you speak in your body's obsession patterns? I say.

And you say, once that's gone, what is there to say? One is then a corpse.

I am a corpse, I say. I have fingerprints but nowhere to put them, or do I even have fingers?

Inside, I say, I trained to be yours. Kissing the cheek of the one who chose not to be real. The feelings seemed deep enough, were they? I accepted your vision; now I can't see. New combinations, purulent and inhumane, ooze from me.

You say that I allow you no character.

Of course not, I say.

I don't remember who, I say, if I'm at a point of transformation. I saw a sun never covered; my only eye. I am the body. I always was, and this moment is anarchic.

There wasn't a reason for the world, I say. It didn't last, because we forced our reasons onto it.

> Out of the bitter plasma
> I'm stretching
> here, out; mirroring

matter to you.

For you.

You have always enjoyed my sufferings; they sufficed for your time. Are you frightened that only you created yourself?

There's no pattern to these old stories; they're not sure when they occur now. The stories that had their own life. Broken loose from my flesh, where are they?

Previously your body was wired, so your innocence or guilt could be overheard. Your body was wired, so you could know that the wires knew.

These words are caked odor in the bone. Can they ever speak again? If world ends, can words speak again? You are lost language, I say. Where was it in this corpse planet, code, code for you?

You say you have to understand why this body is here. Who put it in front of you? Why did time leave you? See the body? you say. It's a stranger now. See the earth? It's also a stranger.

(5)

Now you say to me that my presumptions must be empty. There's nothing here to refer to but a body. Someone must remove it soon. The cops.

There are no cops here. Don't you touch me, I say.

This corpse must be removed to the morgue, you say.

Don't you dare, I say. There's no place to put me anyway.

You think that I'm yours because I'm dead, I say. You want to hide me between your words. Like another lifetime.

All details are still alive, somewhere on earth, you say.

But where is that?

You wanted to see me, you say, in all my portions; to know what they were, to help me. The body shouldn't be a prison to a weak or aging woman. In my details, I had been beautiful, you say.

Oh how can I be interested in that? And I'll walk down the

hallway towards my new door, to live alone. Rising from a broken sun, I'll never have to touch what you see.

You say you merely served me. The true money and the true fact; so practical.

> Keep your facts
> clear, the man said;
> but I can't now. There
> aren't any facts.

I'm supposed to see my cells, my proteins in dissolution; but my dead sight's not interested in them. If I'm the remnant of your details, they fail to signify. I hardly remember you.

You say that you may have murdered me. I say there's no authority, here, for us to tell that to.

You say you dissected me. You saw through me. You planned for my neediness; you learned what you could from my progress in time. You even dressed me.

You say that I'm not that old.

Who cares? I say.

You say that you just want to be in your own story. You owned it, after all.

Now I start to remember who you are. As in details, like the toll on me. I was supposed to sit outside your apartment. Check off your guests' names, as they arrived at your party. You and your symbolic partner. It was supposed to be all right that I wasn't with you. Not a main player, for that evening. Only, really, you.

I became the corpse, because—and then, it floats away again. The line won't hold. But murder was condoned. If it helped your character forward.

You must have killed me sometime that evening. But how can anyone care, with no line or time to reason; and my flesh almost gone?

Don't I want to reconcile? you ask.

Do we know each other now? I say.

They would probably like to compare X-rays and bones, you say, to make an identification.

I say I know who I am. I entered the trailor, this black one, and found it less wanting than the world, where my eyes had filtered outwards and were only part. I didn't want to be a part. Designated by you.

You say that I'm forcing you to kill me. My wish is to ruin things, you say.

I'm already dead, I say, but if I'm the earth or ocean, you have ruined me. If I'm Catherine, it's just a hit. It's all about you, as always. How you can have the importance you deserve, whatever you do.

What was the time of death? you ask. You say that you still don't remember killing me, maybe you haven't done it yet. You've been trying to comprehend why I'm so sad. And now you are too. It must be somewhere in the brain, the endocrine system. Upbringing. You can work on all of that.

You were so excited about someone's research, I say. His return. Your teeth shone showing that you loved him as you spoke. His work made everything clear to you. I didn't accept your clarity.

You say that must have been Mark.

I say, I'm tired of your excitement.

(6)

You say that I had to be less important, because I was. When I insisted on myself, you knew you had to kill me. You say that you don't remember doing that, still.

Mark, you say. Mark's precision inspired you, to search my being. Hasn't the body been identified? You can't find our times, you say.

You needed to prove I wasn't right, I say. I might be the one who was right, if I existed. But if you could cut me. Explore me. Tell me what I meant.

We were just wild animals, you say. As in the theory.

I wasn't, I say. Your knife, your words, your mark.

Tell me, where did you go so wild? you say.

I was the perfect animal? I say. Because all of my parts bled
fluids. Wherever you cut, I reacted. All of my anguish was physical. I had
no soul. You were gratified.

And so I'm not here? I say.

Corpse! you say, that's all it ever was, you say. You can't remember, you say to me, the moment when you killed me.

You'll have to wait for that moment of memory, I say. Here,
moments spiral around and return. Sending out patterns; no linear order,
I say. I'm the light. And the one who begs for it. Amber beads broken
around me. No physics: the wheel won't turn.

My eyes, my heart, my liver. You don't remember in what order
you pierced them. It was very long and sharp.

The minute's flown away again, you say.

The problem with the stories, I say, was that they never happened.
This happened. I witnessed my own murder. You had to deny me, because
of my talent: the earth has a talent, you'd say? Or are you Catherine,
you'd say, whose talent was to die? To follow in footsteps, your
footsteps—is that a talent?

Do you know who's singing this? I say. Do you know who's
always sung it? This is my song. This is now 'the song.'

You say it isn't marked. Is it a song? Mark's thoughts clear,
perfect, were the real song. Didn't I miss him, you say.

Oh I'm dead, I say. But maybe I do.

Now I begin to remember. He was at the party with. You can't see
her— You don't think it's me, you say. He wants to tell us everything he
knows. He's with a woman's name. You can't remember her. I will confront you and tell you. That I'm leaving the experiment. You say no one
can leave it; it has to be true for everyone. Because you have to pretend.
And I'm just a model. Put on those clothes. For my age. Let you find out
why you think I love. You can open me and look within my materials.

But theories break
when you leave
the room
later.

I say I remember walking in a long ermine skirt. An animal? And a dark fur cape. Towards you. The theory says one kills the competition. You are killing me, because I'm more intelligent. Than you. But shouldn't the intelligent win? Not unless they're violent. Did you say that? You are killing me because I know more than your experiment will ever find out. Words—not me but my words. You want to cut them out of my body.

You say you want to kill me right now.

I say, here you have no weapon.

I thought I needed you, I say now. Probably don't. I will walk on down. On this bridge I'm perfect; decaying I'm perfect; unwomanly, unbelieving I'm perfect; alone I'm perfect. Fear it, if you wish. Dance to the music of the tabor and the gun.

You say you were supposed to find out why I loved. You're not sure I did love.

There's no one to love; blind where I've fallen, so full of love. I don't need you any more. I don't need anyone here in order to love.

(7)

I say, in the lightning, I let you kill me. Because you were of no consequence. Neither the murderer nor the police are important.

The earth's soul rises above it; my continual chance. Chances pour in from all sides in no order, stippling my wings. Which are arms. I'm outside an airplane, unprotected by metal, flying.

I had come back, like it was written in my soul.

In the void of love where I always go, I say, where I have never been corruptible. Hear my voice throughout the letter, always. The letter's no longer stable, doesn't surround you, I say. It's Catherine, it's Mark; it's the fact that you killed me. It will never be as you wished.

And I,
I say, I have
gone down the
way.

You ask if I'm not really dead.

You were never supposed to believe your eyes, I say. Do you think that *you* could kill *me*?

You say you yourself are dead; and I say, that's up to you.

This place is no projection, you say.

Why should I ever have cared for your violence, as if it were integral to me? I have gone down the way, again, I say.

I shrug my wing, or angelic hair. For I have gone backwards to young. Before I was broken.

And you, you still have to go down the way.

The wheel was what you never chose to know, because a symbol can't be controlled experimentally.

This is no solution, you say.

I'm flying, I say. This is the physics of symbols, I say. Is it moving you? I fly above it.

This is the motion of what's known too fast for your experiment. This is your mind moving but not under construction.

You could only pin down a corpse. You've dissected the earth, but you've lost it.

It's all in your mind, it's nowhere, it's light, it's memory fast without a home. You can't depend on it or lightning. Everything spoken for has crumbled. The mind trembling, what you sense is your shining commitment—you have to do it without the names now, I say.

You wouldn't have to be here, but you are. Do you still want the plot of the murder, to keep you defined to yourself?

It's built up like shimmering cloth but must be defined by the tolling of a bell. You think. But there's no bell.

And the cloth has no edge, down the way.

You say that you've disappeared into the black trailor. You say that someone will murder you there, in an inaction you can't control, not any more. You can't see another way out.

But there doesn't have to be a way in, a way out. It's over.

And if you're referring to your anguish, it's just a thing. The shape of a trailor, a wheel, or a knife. Leave the details of your life and find another one.

HOUSEHOLD

It was that motel on the railroad tracks side of the road, before it passed on east from the center of town. I can hardly remember how the motel looked; it barely had a look, with athels around it and trains showing through behind them.

I like this one place—and it's still standing—because nothing happened there; I never went inside; I didn't know the owner.

I don't want to relate to someone, though I know a form of address is in process.

But no one else is here, and I write in no stasis, no tension. Most of the people have left the center of town. Businesses have closed because there are greedier ones elsewhere, not far. People live up on the hill and cross the river for their goods. The motel is closed and run-down.

I don't think you should sing like that, for sentiment, your own damn ego. She's at her best, that singer, but there's a lack of cognitive pressure inside her. She values some damn sentiment.

I've come back to where I'm not in relation, except that I'm scratching words down. It's like towards the beginning of my life, but then I was afraid I wouldn't leave lack of relation. To my peers and to the elders and all their feelings and thoughts whose passage or possession I was continually informed of.

I was afraid I might enter that motel alone and forever; but if I do now, I'm not afraid. Though I can't step through that door from here. It doesn't matter where I am, no one's here either.

I think he should just sing. I hope he doesn't say anything in the song. I'd like to see the name of the motel on its sign; if his song could just recall that motel's name, nothing else. I want to see the worn shapes of the letters.

But he keeps singing his righteousness, or else fare thee well my own true lover.

I took the train near the motel, many times, over to the coast. Going east I think I always took the bus; it left from a parking lot behind Front Street. There were people caught up in stories or the accidents of tragedy. I can see them from the bus window as it pulls in on the return; facing each other, shadows in the heat.

By now I, too, know all the stories. They aren't any good. Eating at my body when they aren't real in that story form. What form are they real in? Ask the motel. My form, it says, like anyone.

This motel, you, have been here longer than anyone I know, though you are, and have always been, flimsy and shabby.

I don't think anyone's there any more. Good. If I enter. You have. Everything shabby becomes beautiful if it doesn't blow down. If I'm only a thing, I don't have to be in their feelings, do I?

So I could be here and not need. The food doesn't cost much; and if a person died, she might not particularly register that. It would come and then go.

There are some of those pink-flowered dusty bushes outside. An old heavy metal song passes by. Now that's a good sound here, it's just another thing.

One fact is the power lines, which work except during the annual storm or two. The communicative touch, and I may have to call up someone I don't really know. I can act friendly. I don't want to make anyone unhappy, but I'm not home like they are.

They ask me if I want something from the outskirts of town or the other side of the river. Just the food. And I've got the books here, though I don't read the best ones any more. I don't believe the stories, but I like some disclosures of suffering.

It's a small motel with only six or seven empty rooms. There should be a problem with passing the time, so why isn't there? Because, though the motel exists in time, if you believe in time, it doesn't itself believe.

If I step out on the street and look west, the town's deserted. It's all like me; and any song for this would just be bullshit. This is a thing, where they stopped trying, they deserted it, and desertion itself is the only possible song. The desertion is here, and is something to respect, not for them but for it. It is so beautiful.

Entering the Jewel

If I didn't go where one told me, I wouldn't have a life at all.
Simple.

We were walking towards the Jewel and it was late then, has been
late throughout my times, though the body seems to tell one otherwise
(the body being what we define it—the body—with, though we are
confident as hell).

Did you say I had to go to the Jewel? I was supposed to be
interested in occasions of nourishment; you were sure of this, a woman.
That is all I can remember about entering the Jewel, and that later we
crossed the street and went into another store.

We might have discussed "love," though I can't remember that as
a topic. For you love was that which made you lovable. I feel so battered
by it now, that I can't find its origins anywhere. I suspect you still think
you're the focus of love and somehow that's the same as its source.

You acted as if you loved, but you faced the beloved as if he or she
existed because you loved them. This love was a possession of yours—you
weren't possessed by it, you owned it in order for it to be seen. Most of all
you wanted to be made love to.

That probably isn't true.

He was in a bed with me, but he was an old beat or hippy I didn't
recognize, characterized by kindness. I don't know if kindness is such a
thing; it helps, but are we all related? None of the words work now,
except insofar as they please without having to mean everything they
could. A lot of meanings don't apply.

I don't know about this love. I entered and never left positions of
attachment, though anything tumultuous happened. There is no reason
anywhere.

Someone returns from death for a moment, and everyone says he
is blue, but I can't see the blue. I don't want to keep seeing him, because
I think I'm over it. Over all of it.

I don't blame you for loving only yourself, why not? It has been a
lot of years since we walked towards the Jewel, and I can't see the sense in

one thing. I don't want anyone to die since so many have; but perhaps that won't make sense in the future. I don't want anyone to die; anyone does.

I think you were probably very attractive, but I couldn't see it. Now, for me "attractive" is meaningless, as if I were a newborn. I might as well not know the language; or else I would say you had long hair large eyes, but I'm already bored. I can't see you. I don't want to see in that way.

If you taught me how to cook something, and then how our lives are made up of cooking—or there are trees there though it's dark. I like that they're there but not seeing them. Or a photo of a successful man, why bother with him? He lets grovelers complete him, as if it were love, was that like you? No, there was fear in your need. I have no sincere hopes for either of us, except perhaps that we never be terrified again.

What was wanted by your self-scrutiny? Love, anyone would say, and I caught it between the trees but then dropped it willingly. It was a form of words, but it wasn't a thing. As the fear we felt separately, later, and earlier, was; and the misery that binds me to others, the dead returning at night in their affection. They still love me, I feel it; but that is no golden state. I suppose it really is blue. And that maybe I love you now, since love suffers and recognizes suffering. Maybe in that way I can call myself love. And, at least to the dead, a beloved.

I'm not calling to any of them, though they keep coming to me. Is there an unknowing self, or would that be the one who knows? Knows what? That love persists forever, and death has no power except to serve it, by causing it to flourish more. There is no pain but love-caused, and so what else is there?

If I sound antique, I might as well. It was a sound you liked if either the great dead or yourself were the source. In the ambiance of those twins, the dead poet and you. He will never leave you, because you never knew him; several will leave me. After we've entered the Jewel.

It is red, a neon cast to step into. I will be trying to step out of it ever after; the figures inside don't make sense, and I can never tell if they are real. We are still among them then, but I don't wish to see myself there. I don't ever wish to see myself anywhere.

The Old One

It was always an old self. It was the oldest self so far, but it was also a continuous one. It had once traveled there to be you, and hadn't said what you had to do. Did it say you had a vagina or something? No, it didn't have a history. And each time could have been the first time.

The affluent are doing their verminal thing as everyone insists their budget's broken. Your love is taking a long time to cooperate with these others though you need what they have: money and publication. If you are a genius you might as well not be, because the budget's for hacks and the usual format—discreet pages of poetry; if you are sick you are a clumsy viral personal projection infecting the child.

Each time could have been the first.

This is what you might call a haunted space. Though it came empty and clean once, it knows where we have been blown and how the laws are codified in a fit of repulsion at any new birth.

The flower was so silken and brilliant it had to be set on fire. Every flower you could describe; nothing is good enough for that one there, who wants to own beauty—but is it expensive enough? And if your price is lower than the laureate's, you should be getting even less than you are.

Each time could have been the first one. You write about the first time as often as you are in now. No one knows your purpose, because it isn't to serve rats.

The shadows in this space do tell their sort of truths, and as the world hates poetry and its contempt permeates dealings outside the sane space, with its sane ghosts, the ghosts urge you to honor something, your oldest self. But where is it? Where are her poems if they're not publishable? This was everything that was supposed to happen, because there's no honor—as in honor to the flower.

The old self says to the ghosts, the old old old self: Since you aren't dead enough not to be here, one's demise isn't the truth; this is an Archive of lost poems, and who else but us knows anything now? Any syllable of the prior self which comes from out of nowhere is worth more than a poem by a representative of the institutional holdings.

The monetary holdings are impregnable to many; but one wanted to place one's poems in a safe, the highest federal safe safe, and the ghosts could have hung out there too. The story does change with age and the desperation you feel towards poetry's precariousness intensifies as the petals catch fire, which were orange to begin with.

You know he absolutely knows that it—the poem—is too long. If only you wouldn't stay on so long, really, an older and older one.

Each time could have been, but this is the dark eye of the oldest self. The oldest self knows it is betrayed by the others, the oldest self isn't supposed to care, because it's the oldest self but it's also the self who recognizes its betrayal. How can that be? Why isn't it too pure to register ordinary betrayal? It is so pure it registers all betrayal.

And the ghosts in this space see through and through, and the oldest self with her first dark eye will allow nothing now without a return of honor. It is the original.

In Forgetting

Because he took that strange girl on his knee. One might kill them, because people kill.

Do you remember? Or it could be any loving thing. Why read the murder book, when it's a lie except for the death?

But you can enter any false world and be in it truly.

I remember no one's fine eyes; I remember no one's large heart. No one I've known or am can either find or understand.

I'm entering forgetting; is there a story in forgetting?

I can say betrayal and remember nothing. He will leave her in the nature of things as spoken for. I have never been allowed to invent the nature of things, but now I will. I will betray you.

Walking too far north.

I want to leave not as a martyr but in strength, not admit that they're singing. If they're singing behind my back.

The girl places her loaf of pudding on the ground.

You sing so poorly with him. You make him sing off-key.

I walked north or flew. I flew. I flew on more and more northward. I've gone too far but I know where I am.

I see bodies in the snow, as I walk out, but I'm dead myself. The entire north knows this. He took the manitou on his knee and I succumbed. So why read the murder book? The only real murder is mine.

As I fly above the white north. Wonder who's dead and if their souls will appear.

Everyone in this land is a frozen eyeless heartless forgetting.

One might recognize the form of someone you knew; you won't know if this one recognizes you. You may not know exactly what recognition is, if they have killed you.

Well someone has. Do you care who killed you?

There is a walrus-like man, a silkie, in the night exchange coming towards me. He walks upright and would like to say something, but the counter-exchange is formless; my words are lost.

I'm now not a born and raised being.

I may be searching for the betrayal, but the word is too obscure to keep shape. I see her but I know I'm not looking for her.

It's interesting her eyes are torn places. That was always a possibility.

Who did this?

Was she untrue once or did she witness it?

No one will find you again.

Was I to be found or to find?

She still can't see through those eyes, and one suspects she would howl if there were any sound here; but all sound is internal.

He sits her on his knee. Their child leaves her mouth, but it is a saying I quickly forget: *my lie will mean as much.* Did she say that?

I'm going on past those ones.

Are you looking for injustice?

Justice and injustice are equally cold; hate can't be suppressed though, what is it?

I think it is something inside, from the sky. It can't be buried in the ground.

No murderer can be discerned, not by looking; but I think I might be my lost eyes. Only those.

Is there anywhere else you'd like to be?

Don't come see me; but I will see you.

I'm flying over the port of kayaks. In you it is no longer. I see letting it go.

This must be the betrayal—seeing.

GOD HAS MONEY

It's so money. Do you really think you can find anything but that in your unconscious? Can you prove a different thing? Every discomfort confronts it. Every piece of your appearance.

I hugged her but she pointed to my hair. The cut is cheap; it grows out with no care, and someone younger watches from a car, going on towards the money. Not a whole lot, but if you can't distinguish yourself from the products who live on the street, called the less.

She doesn't like you; she has moved up. She has a position. And each poem, fruit from the temptress; saying, this one earns now. I haven't seen her for awhile except in my unconscious. I lost track of my days and found myself alone—no money. But if I never moved from this seat, would I need it?

It is confused as to why people are in motion. They seem to need payment from each other. Can he find a position inferior to money in the rain of the hallway, where he's allowed to sleep? Moved back in with his mother; because he had nowhere left. He shouldn't have spent it on drugs; he should have spent it on cash.

An allowance is being made out to you, the better than a junky. You think you are superior to your former, poisoned self, but it's often hard to say. You think you did worse things to people when you damaged them individually, not as a force for governance. Nothing you do being so apparent now, the world outside your borders in its silence.

Every one of his muscles, each centimeter of her cunt, a payback for having grown up. That much is affordable. A stack of checks I thought were mine were not; there is the supposed checkpoint where you may be too old to earn, having no apples to sell.

Every reason why you might stand naked before others. You can't buy the garments: though they have been taken or lost; why haven't you replaced them, starting from the thread? Which anyone can buy.

If I had more money you'd love me still. He had the most because music counts—it soothes you while you work for them—composed of his projected talents.

I had many dreams about loss, everyone gone to the mechanism, that would obliterate your poverty, if you'd succumb to morality, a monetary force. But as these delicious words slide over the tongue, I wonder how I achieved them, without paying, except in blood? A song soaked in it, that no one wants to sing; their preference remains the glorious sins of the master. He alone suffered, because he has enough wealth to tell you so. And will never let you go.

IN THE GARDEN

Did you ever see that movie, Ted said, who knows what words he used? It was about the TVA, in the 30s; Montgomery Clift is the TVA man, who enters a remote community to do—whatever, and has a romance with Lee Remick. So, at the end, she poles him back across the river, because he's done and he's leaving her, and then she's alone in the boat, or raft, going home, and she sings "In the Garden." The hymn. Which begins, "I come to the garden alone." With the refrain, "And he walks with me/ and he talks with me/ and he tells me I am his own . . ."

It had been my father's favorite hymn, so I sang a bit of it to Ted. Then he said he'd never forget Lee Remick singing that song, so simply; and now I can always see and hear it too, though I never did. I'll never forget it.

I recently bought a CD of Elvis Presley singing devotional songs. I wanted to hear "Peace in the Valley," and found "In the Garden" there too, in this collection of rather austere, mixed-race gospel. The feeling in his voice is true, esthetic but awed, in its purity of musical heart.

"Peace in the Valley" was sung at my brother's funeral, by a man we all knew, a former coach and gym teacher. He accompanied himself on the guitar. Before the service the family members were alone together, at a long table in a room to the side of the church. I broke down in there and had to be comforted by my mother. "If you want to know who feels the most for each other, it's the sisters and brothers," she said.

The day before, we had all been at the viewing in the mortuary, no longer run by the family that had tended to everyone's remains while I was growing up. I sat next to my uncle, who was caught by how my mother was standing: "She looks like my mother," he said. I remember she was wearing a skirt, which she hardly ever did anymore, and her legs looked vulnerable, thin, a lot like Grandma's. Then my uncle became upset; and he later said he'd heard my brother's voice calling out to him: "Bill! Bill!"

These are the same stories as always, and I almost understand them hearing the songs; the religious feeling becomes connected less to a god, than to shapes for grief stripped to shape alone.

If you can see that shape in its simplicity, you can live in it. I come to the garden alone, and there's no one there; that's better. There was no one in the boat with her, as she poled back across the river.

INSIDE

I let them all inside me.

His mind never changed about me, I know.

He was true. But do I have to hear these sayings forever?

Listen. He says. I don't want to be by your skin. I just want you to know.

But I know. I don't think the dead should be sentimental. But now I don't know which one you are.

She said the door to our household was too open, wide open. She said I had to protect myself more.

I dressed in earrings as if to say I was a member of a culture, though I never knew which one.

He came to visit while I was out and told you he was now a strongman for the mafia. I think I remember him sitting there when I returned.

He had once knocked you down and broken your glasses, as you stood outside our door. Before we were friendly with him.

Because he hadn't entered?

But when they enter, they do a different thing, becoming permanent voices in here, until I am mad with guilt, because I wasn't large enough to heal you—them.

Oh, you too—singing the shapes of the heart in green eyes.

Can I still use these voices? My diagram of self as alone.

Anything I say to myself might be any of you. A voice of yours. There are others.

You say you're looking for someone, alive now in the future.

I say I'm looking for someone.

It's all memorized.

But it never knows when it will come, how it will say it.

And anyway I'm not alone.

Doesn't anyone die? Doesn't any scene dissolve?

No you are condemned to know us, for we were like that. And none of us will ever forget you.

Come in I'll give you shelter. I'll give your being and voices shelter, I'll rub this rain into your dryness, within an enclave of care.

IMMIGRANTS

You were the immigrant weren't you. What else would I be. It was the first thing I always was after whatever I can't remember, she said. She said this because one is set up to speak. You think she's yours, for example; you don't know anything about her. I've immigrated into so many places and situations, she was saying, never being sure of which one. Which one what? I asked. Which one was my destination; no one is born to stay where the birth was any more; but it's even harder to conceive of a true destination. I've gone with the man several times to certain places, but certainty was only an aspect of love or disillusion. Here in this country I still have no book to quote from except the book of previous countries—Do you want such a book?—I don't know how to want. Maybe you don't have to. She then gestured so we would know we were of our milieu, but I think she was saying that reference was meaningless to her. Do I do it for others or myself? I know the answer's both. Pick up the glass of perrier. I can't find you, she said to no one in particular, and not to me. The head scarf issue might be worth discussing; or the serial killer and prostitutes in Toulouse. But, it's not that—I don't live in another world, but this one's shifty. The drunken man is at the wheel, everywhere, and no matter what I say or do he stays there. I don't want to be in his car, because I don't know where he's "immigrating to" next and he is he who chooses our illusion. I asked if she thought he should die, of course she said, and I would kill him myself if he could become as concentrated into his essence as I have, as I lose everything, my connections, and so do know. Much of communion should take place in the form of a curse. I don't pity him or us, she said, while I had a sudden memory of a time spent beneath the ground. My birth but had I ever been born? The suppressor of birth, is that an aspect of everyman? Someone hands me a chain of bone, as if to condition my resurrection. I may accept that necklace, if it's towards the power of destruction. I would kill too, I say to her. I would welcome his entrance next time he sees me in the place where he wants to stand; in my space I can kill. There is no destroyer but me, and there are no ancient godly forces, for they purport to be him. For myself I am the creator, the sustainer, and the destroyer. The routes of my immigration are over.

I don't want them at all, she said, but tolerate the sound. I mean the names for living forces. They are insane: volition, pleasure, economy. To shake someone's hand because he has explained that to greet him gives one access to his force. I remember all of this from when I first saw true, but I remember again and again as women shrug at me. One could say to them, None of you know again; your little clothes proclaim it. That isn't nice where my love and I have laid; what I experience is the violence of ripping the pretty chains, one too many days and not enough death-black nights for you yet, and by the time you do see you'll be weak and unable to concentrate.

At my door the leaves lie dead, but I don't have a door. I don't miss anything and I don't wonder about anything; I took the remnant of blood from some victim's temple—where it bled through the gray hair, and smeared it on my own forehead. It didn't matter; what's at the very bottom? Where they drank the blood? The old gods of your urge to control and now you've added my blood to the storehouse of guilt that props up the vehicle and map? Do I want my blood to have been good for something better than your projects? I don't want my blood "to have been good for" anything.

A story can't be told, she said; no it can't. Make nothing of this; to be this negative is an action with no known flower yet, but I prize it, I said.

This Plot

It is a case of dislocation, getting separated every night. It was happening in several geographical directions—sometimes I couldn't find them again after we'd set off towards Europe; but back in New York I was rushing downtown. Trying to rejoin the beloveds.

This plot will always dissolve, I will always be its fool. Someone hands me my medicine, but not because I am beautiful or worthy. That is why I live here.

It's like Siberia today, the pharmacist said.

The other places where I might go aren't very far. I might walk as far as the Boulevard Magenta later. I'm reading a book in English but I'm skipping most of the words, which are inconsequential to the plot. So many of the words I've read this year don't matter.

In the pharmacy I was uncertain about a word. My medical treatment is working so am I *recepteur*? *recepteuse*? No, *receptive*. It's a language of fools she said.

My most mysterious involvement is with speaking; but mysteries transpire at night because they're obvious though can't be anticipated.

Where are the people I love? Where am I? No one is where she thinks she is, and there is no absolute geography. I don't believe you are anywhere. I never know when I'll discover that I can't find you, that you aren't here. Or that somehow you are.

Two were alive and one was dead but they were together and I became separated from them, initially at an airport, then on a highway, then later awake through the day. I won't find you in any of these books, so what good is prose?

There is a mind I don't want to be in. I want my own. Where is it? There is no where. But I connected with another at the pharmacy today: Mme. Caizergues who has always been so kind.

Conspiracy

It's a conspiracy, because everything is; that's the way you believe in things with others.

Then it's a letdown, a joke. They've gone and left you.

Where are the violent? Did you ever hit anyone?

The middle classes don't believe in fate; the middle classes believe in objects bought.

They can't tell a story without an appliance or a fabric.

He came down the gone way. He used to buy a lot of stuff, and he was so full of hurt he bought three, three of the same thing always. They later told him this was addictive behavior. That was their bullshit not his.

I seen you when you was a kid.

They found a hand in a plastic bag, floating in the river.

This is reactive, but I don't know what to. They keep saying 'hard-wire,' 'mind-set,' etc.

She said she walked into that house, and there was a body sitting in a chair, a corpse. The guy acted like everything was normal; she didn't tell anyone for awhile. So she told the addicted guy and others later. Everyone believed that that man, the one with the corpse in his house, might have cut his girlfriend up into pieces. The hand in the river.

For a long time they acted like he was a serial killer. He worked in a gas station. He still works there, and I don't know who to believe.

Are any of these people in the middle classes?

I would say no, but that doesn't mean the middle classes win.

How far into fantasy do you go with others in your life? My therapist said of the hurt, addicted man who always bought extras, he isn't going to die. But a few years later he did—I mean, her fantasy was that they don't die. He wasn't addicted to drugs at the time. I didn't know what was wrong, but I had a strong feeling about him, and I was afraid he was fated. In effect she said that's your fantasy. She was middle-class; and he did die.

This is an object. Where? What? I don't know what an object is anymore. Is it like a tone of voice? If you buy three, you don't get to have the class thing.

A man in prison has confessed to killing a girl from the same town. They've finally found her body. This killing happened around the same time as the alleged other murder—the cut-up corpse. No one knew where this girl was buried for over twenty years.

I keep trying to be delicate. I'm not telling everything.

I really live in another country. I keep in touch.

I wanted to be famous, but I might as well have wanted to have extras of everything. I might as well have been him.

They named the little league park for the girl, over twenty years ago, though no one knew where her body was then. They just knew she was dead.

No one is clear about the woman to whom the hand belonged. I can't find anyone who'll tell me who she was. No one seems to remember if there really was a hand.

LOCUST

If you come here I might see you.

I'm looking for another you or story. Your wings are moist, you have dark eyes and sing.

To dis-haunt oneself, stay away from old fires. The only exorcism, the buzzing of the arrival.

You are holding out a gift. You're edible, but aren't we all. You survive the lightning bolt because you are small.

You can occupy the new land, because there is something small about you.

So it can be June. There's larkspur in the closed eye.

Maybe I was too tried.

Can I bring it, a handful of story, that isn't known? It doesn't have to fit into any shape. Good. It doesn't have to have hips.

Only the buzzing can tell me.

Soon I'll ask the quail what it ever did. Did you swallow medicine? I'll sing.

Yellow flower, don't get jealous of her.

I heard this buzzing, that's all I know. I saw your eyes. This is the place of tolerance.

They talk about fertility. Or a guarantee of survival. They started to talk like that so they could kill the people.

The insect singer is in danger; the insect may know a spell. Stay away from old fires.

What if the flowers across the land aren't beautiful? This year they burned.

You usually wear the sun yourself, and as you are small, it isn't too large.

This year they stole it and made it large. They wanted a huge sun to rise. They said, this would be new. Oh, it is. Where is my story?

Printed on a wing.

A hundred pieces glued back together make one wing. I now have two.

Open your ear.

Three-times modern don't leave us, or we will die. A thousand times modern don't leave us.

There is no evidence.

A ceremony makes the world warm. Too many ceremonies make the world too warm.

There is no evidence.

There is another story, inside a drop of spit. I see it.

The river is ruined.

I still see it. But I can't tell just anyone. They are becoming more and more unfamiliar.

Among them I have no likeness. What was once mine.

They have created a fantasy, because they have all the details.

But they can't sing.

It just comes out of a buzz. Just say the words.

I went there, in their midst. Perished and came back to life.

Do you think sound could die?

Do you think these sounds could die? So far they come back to life again.

But do you think they could die?

HEMOSTATIC

HEMOSTATIC

He wanted to know what blood was for.

Who is of interest when the water gets low? Or,
Does blood wish to be in a seaport town?

Would it have to be another *he*?

Is it interesting when the older ones shed theirs?

I once found a city for several years.
Perhaps we founded it, down where it pumped.

And I was sure of my worth.

Someone could die. Before they
Anyone, left me here facing your walls.
Each minute where nothing seems to circulate.

This is a red ride without
And maybe you can't know me now.

Maybe I'm just blood.
Whatever that's for.

Our Violent Times

We had our violent times
        now in these ones
we have more. No one's against
      it,
Violence is almost not this
No one's movies, books, the
      story

of how we get by. Not against
her personal country's revolution.
Now we have more   Everyone's
      cold
around within an exterior mind

Too hot, too cold.   It would be good,
      too,
if you could be prior, in some ways
The ways we were used to you
before just before now blew you
      away. I,

the one I know, will leave again
Forgetting forms, the pieces fall
      of a membrane of rags.

LaDonna

I'm searching for the child,
calling out her name *LaDonna*!
Walking through rooms in anywhere at all

Calling out her name, LaDonna
throughout rooms anywhere at all.

I don't know who you are anymore.

I don't know who I'm talking to

who's left who, or who's left

there's no poem in my
house, where is LaDonna, LaDonna!

The little girl had looked at me reproachfully
when I left her temporarily
to get some Relief. Studying police procedurals

I lost my lady.
Curse you with your legal violence
your contractual allegory of possession

Where is LaDonna, LaDonna, my lady, my child?

When You Could Hear Them All the Time

when you could hear them all the time
but there was nothing to say
except for Love Me—I wrote those songs
you're supposed to be.

the formation of victory approached

it was sinister   is there a
        metallic
turn   can you hear it in
your,   that,   past?   he put
        it there   who?

preacher you,

shores of odious see-it-that-way,
this species happily dies for that
so he sings once again, it's not me.

it's all somewhere else. no one lives in a country.

THE GIRLS

I stayed home and cleaned up the remains of his mess.
I'm talking to you, he said, but I knew he wasn't.
The girls thought they had it covered now—
pieced accusatory language, worn with the usual
clothes. So if his spittle is wrong for the drink
I'm listening to his songs, all the way back from
the stores where he earns rave notice.
Still yourself? the dead person asks, laughing.
As I'm not there, I'd say, but there are certain
rhymes. Are they my content
Why do you protect it? I am their power—'to Show'
                    Did you
did you, did someone teach it to teach you? Even if
she was glitter silver, on her pregnant hair
in black velvet. Couldn't see that I was running
from my killers, all along the purple heather.
                    Will you go?

My Lady Shadow

My lady shadow I'm stumbling away
opening locks. Did you think
I wanted to burn on a different
wheel? She turns her head to the left
and will have no name. She asserts not speaking.
I'm going from this hallway I reply.

A harmonica can burn you too
any good can wound. Leaving, I'll miss you
from whom I can accept nothing angelic
a fixed vow precluding illusions
I don't know who I can be, but
you can't give it to me. Yet I'm talking to you.

Are you still yourself, he'd said sarcastically
knowing I was not. Can I glimpse you
abandoning everything yours except that
little sound, surrounding your wordless core?
I've caused much to happen to me
but was never quite that woman. I thought of you

not a fetish; a shade of stone, like myself
I know your texture—*Are you still yourself? he said*—
You are, not me.
                    Facing well the ladyless
path—or is the other a woman we both
don't recognize? And wheel, not desire,
purely to turn and convey me. Left, I'm the way.

Dialogue in the Glass Dimensions

If I tell you
                    you're suffering,
          will you believe me?
                              down in the
glass retreating   or up on the peak?

Where I'm always   cutting my hair, I sing.

I narrate your path to you,
You say you're tired of the price.
Why are the pictures hung upsidedown?
Why are you in this room?

I didn't ask to be

if I turn them around   I see
they're supposed   to be me. They—
the lock may be damaged
   I don't need locks now
I mean luck.   They—
     the house comes down—
don't fully describe my bad luck.

Photos of isolated   parts of blownup
          bodies
esthetic objects. Is that the suffering? No

I was once destroyed
and now can only focus on

boded re-   sults in this hook. I
sing, the   victim child. Must I

keep on their   path so long a-
go I on-   ly remember
parts.

      Can they be   beautiful?

I entered the format then.
But   there's no story   any-
  more.
      I'll show you
how I rescued you
where the path turns.

            I don't care
what you've done
        for me.
Swaying on stage,
        just that,
isn't it enough?

not to try to
return   to a place that is
story's

beginning: to destroy my-
self for others   sees it from child-
hood. Keep on path   I don't want to
remember   any parts at
all. Each child   has a separ-
ate appoint-   ment. It's her own
to remem-   ber or not. I

stare at my-   self in the glass
below. So   I can impose
discipline.   I've been in train-

ing forev-   er. Up on moun-
tain it's worse   where I balance
on the glass.

Why do you still act   as if there's something?

Not even what I've gone through?

but it's an-   y old story,
whatever   field of parts. If
you think this   is a passage
to now. Am   I supposed to
move you? There's   neither the so-
cial, nor the   individual,
body: I saw her   at the corner.
This dust of   dead insects
in her mouth   is obvious.

But I, the narrator,   don't believe her. I don't
believe my own luck,   as bad as your serial
parts left strewn   along the glass palace walls.

I face it for you
                        sing with voice thick
this meter inhales
                        After detonation
it stands

        someone presses to
        the glass at bottom
        crying up and down
        the dimensions. There's
        no up bringing, or
        nature. It was all

locks. In this pro-
fession I sing:
were you lucky to
be born?

            That's only
traditional, a patriarch's question—I
narrate to discount that.

                    But I'll
        face it, in the brave
        meter, tone I be-
        come. What nothing to
        lose is

this body   part you survey
dry old blood   yellowed skin
closed up, sculp-   tural thing.

                            It might
                            blind
us. Are you   singing in the
square?

            I am   obsessed, they say.
Obsessed has no   value. Psychol-
ogy studies   the butterfly
in its own   glass

Your voice is
            stripped down to
its enterprise
of sound.
            Can you move
now?

I can move.
I can walk on the stage.

We can move.

The Portion Accruing to Ears

I know, from its primacy
shadow follow down over European
clutch of tones the same
I know shadow or clutch. so,

whatever is told to you, no waiver
I was there. you can say
nothing accrues in safety   and no one safe
why should you be, or make sense?

all she wore was lace. why not?
or something else. treason, why not?
quote, the only thing I'm sure of, a
       kind of metric
but that thought don't I see, gone and for-
give. You do not have a light
to shine on me. I have it.

I Can't Speak to You

the she. this one, pending surgery

                                Because if

I can't identify with an entire
assigned pronoun throw it in the
                    Ocean. When she
was born, when your sister was.
I can't speak this language.
Inside the devil is your mouth—
I can't speak this language. Does
no one fear it this much? No
pronoun shakes like body. No
way to show such wretchedness,
unless you promise not to fear it.
I can't promise that. Handprint of grease & shit.

To Preachers

There are preachers everywhere
in black rags, playing poker
This is the way where I used to live
I won't greet them down in the remains
you keep warm.

I'm playing
a metric of sense
to you   You can't hear

When have you ever heard
a tone that would require
          the crossing of a line?
I tell you it is unpleasant
          but natural

Like rising from the dead
                              which I did
                              without you

They sent thee out from their old body,
and thou hast been rendered new

YOU HAVE NO IDEA

you have no idea what you do to me
she was clinging to a faceless scapula
they greet you and use that for your warrant

arrested. wake up wondering guilty of what?
I'm supposed to think I want to be in love.
you have no idea what you do to me

howling out your injunctions love and be loved
they didn't have that word when I was an animal
the dead come and get you for sex so you'll scream.

"will I just be dead or will there be something?"
you're the dead man, you should know
you're asking because you still don't know, do you?

it was the kind of sex where I suffer
just like I am supposed to
because that is what I am doing

why can't you stop doing that?
I can't find my house
everything's gone. or it's moved

I don't want it, do I
you have no idea what you do to me

TO THE POEM

I need some light in my right shoulder.
My hand remembers you, writing.
I ask, what's been going on? I
have to write it down. Next to a tamed
Cerberus is where we are.

This is my body, they say: but no man
knows my name; the powerful
homicide lieutenant, or any one character type
will continue to gun down someone's
potent trees. I've lost track of who to notify.
          Is this that?

Even in the fallow, there's no one to implore,
'See for me.' It's my eye—and with back to wall
it's still mine. I don't even hear the voices
in which I could fall down, just to be rescued by man.

The Main Offense

It could be in one's flesh, probably is.
Whatever you are, as born; as well as
the disease you might carry.

String me along, anyway, in case.
You might get something out of me
I could be like your bag man,
if you use my words right. Poetry
can justify you too.

I went up to him and put my hand
on his chest. Why bother healing
such a huge abscess? Do we have
anything in common? You are a
mean bastard; I just write things down.

They made me up for the part
But I grew both into and away from it.
        If there's
something you can't reach, I used to try
to do it. Now I don't know where my
primal loyalty lies. I think it
can't lie. I kind of wish you were dead,
but that's death, isn't it?

In the Circuit

In the circuit
of shades and transit; in the circuit
of shadowed transit whose
paths are sensitive,
patterned, and rational as
if they knew;

When her love felt cold, but
knowledgeable
That design existent almost without me,
in my free instant
But you'll never know about her;

While I slept
affecting my most obscure
fatelines,
from the beginning,
when I, you say, followed him;
Crossing over into
unknowns
neither he nor you could guess;
from my youth's first risks
and still not articulate or conscious;

I've now spoken for many who
spoke to me
We've changed what we could;
But if you don't know you were fated
can you know how light you are?

I'm still going barefoot and so are my dead

SONG

time
lies down

while old dead man
does not arise but is transformed

into a
younger woman. as the birth dew is shed she

arises.
and what shall you do?

I will go to Baltimore, or Tours.

Somebody who knows nothing
is in charge. I mean
but *I* can't *mean*

that no one and nothing is

you will have
daily confrontation   it would
like to hurt your business

in a small room. though

No one's in; and there is no charge

nothing's not in charge and there's

no principle. do you hear

and what's that in your no-
where eyes? why that's not it. Lady

tell what happened where there was
no one. In this song. No one in

charge
appeared, and
time lay down

CULTURE SCARF

I could plead details, skim it
The question: Who did I, no why
(giving into the forms again, sister).
I froze because I was cunt, cruise
through the mud. Jump start
and fake it, like any witness. No way to
                                                    wake up
This is all true writ. records
Shattered: Indicate my dirty
little street. You have always, no shit,
                                                    showed me
Was passive, be back for it. Sure
Wipe the piece, for you. Can make
                                        me
talk. Links would work. You could count
                        your favorite
numbers. Everywhere your ass leads
back to tricks; I'm vaporized chick,
a logical penance: Put it on my fucked
                                        head.

BENEATH YOU

Because there's no   sky through the
                          aperture
City. Call me   cooze. You've placed the
meaning in a   drop. It's just an-
other drop.
                   She isn't to-
gether, like you.

What is there   beneath you?
                       Colors
the form. I   believe that there are
some forms, you   said. I don't for
I'm too tired to   get away with
                             it.

In my crushed-out   eyes I beautifully

     turn   into a moment
that stands for   it. in my crushed-
out eyes the city's   gone. arising
                       moments
flickering   beneath you.

any time I   had to die. be-
neath you in   my eyes.

working for you my-
self. which took lives

in this crushed-out room where
all times come, between the
spokes of my broken irises
there's no one who can sing like me.

they say that I'd   kill, so I could
sing.
        allowed where
the voice pours out for broke.

And you have witnessed my mad scenes

I am unscrupulous to live them.
Isn't this one?

I met him in the curse, didn't
        ELEMENT

I will sing you through your
        mad scene
says
a
voice of it.
                NO DECIPHERMENT

We are working on the translation but
we can't find your body   it's because I
don't believe in forms.
See see love
I won't see a thing.

when you fol-   low me down, to
beneath you.   do you like to

do that, babe? try it on eyes
you have try-   on eyes. Come on
down beneath   you.

BUT WE CAN'T FIND YOUR BODY

I can hardly hear her.
         forms are being
banished; if   you thought you had
glamour. There   was no day that
you didn't re-   fuse to listen.

a factor in the blood, no
  there isn't

all you heard was

Sending it to you, but who?

I can hardly hear her

Rushes up   to you with a
proposition.   This is the busi-
ness of death He will buy your
meat though it's ill. voice rise
         above

start obeying your epitaph.
Just sing through the whole thing. I
walked my blood   towards the forms of
meathooks. in   the dark cages.

this is as   true as
else, you want to   see.

Does the voice   have to reach *up*?
hear this ap-   portioned talent,
voice it, the lady's   name, never.
                        naked, there

they took her clothes

                        her names and
rings. *I know*   *this one*. They took
my time and sold   it for meat; they
will take you too.

                        And you will suffer
under the law of   *I know this one*.

they wanted me so bad.
to sing to their idol
during all the lost days
when time was called special.

I'm supposed to remember,
hung up, how they were
kind. and sing their gross
notes from this mouth.

But if they say   what you did, that
isn't what   you did.

Oh my inno-   cent child
where does your   voice explode from
But if they say   what you did, that
isn't what   you did.

In the court,   you will simper
everyone does.   sucking up to the
                    power
and this is where   you must perform
I remember   those times in some
jurisdiction   stamped on his ass.

I don't want   them breaking it up
I am the   only one who knows
this river of   head throat
navel; on the   hook up its ghostly
current of I

who flows

They'd like you   to report for
a velvet boast   a journal;
safe in our times.

What did I   do?
                 And if I didn't
do it, was   nothing done? Who did
this to me?

                      you got
the replacement   so it would be
in my nature.
          I don't   know why pathos
is your twin   it will not re-
place any-   one

You got the   replacement so
it would be   in my nature

Hand it on   gladly you say.

But I've on-   ly been in the
country for   six weeks. I've on-
ly been here   on this corridor-
boat just to   be somewhere.

Where SURVIVE   is screamed at
                         you by
exchequers'   sons. Mimicry,
wherever   windows are. Go

and I will be   in this long sound.

And too anxious   severing pitches
where memories   aren't that
                     natural
                         later
courageous   to let down your guard?
it's so pale   anyway

over the toss   and if I never
know, what   difference then?

Change fleeing

over the washed-out places
I fell in love with, singing.

                Could I?
                Does one?
and if you say yes,   are you someone?

ABOUT THE AUTHOR

Alice Notley was born in Bisbee, Arizona, on November 8, 1945, and grew up in Needles, California. She was educated at Barnard College and at The Writers Workshop, University of Iowa. During the late sixties and early seventies she lived a peripatetic, rather outlawish poet's life (San Francisco, Bolinas, London, Essex, Chicago) before settling on New York's Lower East Side. For sixteen years there, she was an important force in the eclectic second generation of the so-called New York School of poetry. She has never tried to be anything but a poet, and all her ancillary activities have been directed to that end. Notley is the author of more than thirty books of poetry. Her book-length poem *The Descent of Alette* was published by Penguin in 1996, followed by *Mysteries of Small Houses* (1998), which was one of three nominees for the Pulitzer Prize and was the winner of the *Los Angeles Times* Book Award for Poetry. Recent publications include *Disobedience* (Penguin, 2001); *Coming After: Essays on Poetry*; *Grave of Light: Selected Poems 1970–2005*; and *Alma, or The Dead Woman*. She also edited, with Anselm Berrigan and Edmund Berrigan, *The Collected Poems of Ted Berrigan*. She is a two-time NEA grant recipient and the recipient of a General Electric Foundation Award, a NYFA fellowship, several awards from The Fund for Poetry, and a grant from the Foundation for Contemporary Performance Arts, Inc. In April of 2001, Notley received The Shelley Memorial Award from the Poetry Society of America, and in May of 2001 she received an Academy Award in Literature from the Academy of Arts and Letters. She now lives permanently in Paris.

Printed in the United States
by Baker & Taylor Publisher Services